POLITICS AND MEDIA IN SOCIETY

POLITICS AND MEDIA IN SOCIETY

Discovering the Truth in an Era of Deceit and Disinformation

WILLIAM M. FRASER

ISBN: 978-1-952134-02-9

STAY IN TOUCH WITH WILLIAM

Follow William on Facebook

https://www.facebook.com/William-M-Fraser-104423254412008/

Join my mailing list and get your FREE book, plus all the latest updates, news, freebies, fun, and new book releases!

https://BookHip.com/VDFZJV

This book is dedicated to all those dauntless philosopher kings out there who never cease in their due diligence to preside over a society of justice and truth.

This book takes an in-depth look at the current state of American politics and how the public and media both interact with the political process. It is not the intended purpose in writing this book to take any one particular side or try to convince the reader of the veracity of one opinion over the other. This book simply serves to convey the facts and explain complicated political and social issues that are currently affecting our country. Just think of it as your helpful compass and hopefully enlightening guide through the murky waters and turbulent political storm that is taking shape on the horizon.

Thank you for reading!

CONTENTS

INTRODUCTION

Our Polarizing Politics

OUR PERSONAL VIEWS OF politics have always been a polarizing subject to discuss. The old adage does indeed advise us not to talk about religion or politics in polite company—that is at least if you want to keep that company polite! However, whether we heed that advice or not the polarization of political viewpoints has incrementally increased throughout the years.

And now even the most optimistic of political pundits would most likely tell you that the state of the nation is hopelessly divided when it comes to our opinions and our politics. According to the experts who research this sort of stuff for a living, we all appear to be living within vast echo chambers. What does that actually mean?

An echo chamber is any medium that takes one person's view and incessantly repeats the tenants of it until that lone viewpoint is echoing with resounding intensity while drowning out any opposition. In these situations, both constituents and their political representatives are adamant that they are right on any given topic and immediately dismiss anything to the contrary.

Just take climate change for example. If the winter season is particularly mild, those who support the idea that Earth is getting warmer can be found screaming from the mountaintops that they were right all along. This supposed "evidence" of global warming will then send a resounding echo across social media saying that climate change is more dire than ever, all due to the latest anecdotal reports used to make that argument.

Only later on however might someone point out that there were already much warmer winters, which occurred way back in the 1850's. So much for the imminent threat of global warming! Nevertheless, through the power of online echo chambers, what otherwise would have been an isolated fluke managed to become irrefutable evidence of something much more dire.

Yes, in many ways the Internet has served as the greatest echo chamber of modern times. Just take Facebook for example. The world's largest social network is designed to bring people together. It wasn't really designed for folks to engage with those they disagree with so that they can have spirited and potentially ugly debates with each other. It's designed so that we can get online and easily connect with like-minded people who think and feel the same way that we do.

Facebook helps facilitate the ingathering of groups that can form a narrowly defined circle of influence and opinion. Birds of a feather certainly do tend to flock together, and the power of 'friending' and 'unfriending' those birdies on Facebook streamlines this process even further.

Of course it's fine to have a group of friends that share interests, but social media has such a polarizing power of dividing people and developing tribalized clusters of mentality, that one has to wonder if such tools are hastening political division and polarization like never before. Well, the Russians for one certainly seem to think so!

Because according to Robert Mueller's much vaunted recent report on the Russia Probe; Facebook was a favorite tool of the Russian intelligence operatives in their efforts to manipulate and further divide the American public.

And during the 2016 Presidential election, Russians posing as Americans effectively seeded the Internet with fake accounts mentioning a myriad of controversial topics that were intended to further inflame the temperament of the average American voter. Just about any given article or video at any given time was crawling with a veritable army of Russian bots.

Whether it was Russians pretending to represent Black Lives Matter, Russians advocating issues for LGBTQ, or Russians pretending to be a Pro-Life group in Oklahoma—Russian meddlers were covertly at work on the web.

The prolonged probe by Mueller and company made it clear that in the 2016 election, Russians were wading knee-deep in the hot button issues of the electorate. And unbeknownst to most of us at the time, they were doing their utmost to manipulate various factions of American life and pit people against each other.

When the investigation concluded, there was no actual evidence that Trump or his staff actively colluded with anyone. Russia was simply messing with all of us on a grand scale, and completely of their own accord. And to what end? Well, it seems that some in Russia would like nothing more than to make our nation as divided, chaotic, and polarized as possible.

From Russia's perspective, having a U.S. overwhelmed with internal strife would be a net benefit, since it would essentially make our nation a weaker player on the global stage. The more divided we are—the better for them. That's not to say that the Russians created all the tensions that exist in American politics today; to be clear, in America's ongoing culture wars, we created the animosity ourselves a long time ago.

But some very smart and crafty analysts in Russia have taken note of the fault lines in American society and have figured out how to use mediums such as Facebook (our own personal echo chambers of polarized thought) and they have expertly exploited these platforms to their full advantage.

And according to Mueller's own report, the very fact that we have a president being investigated and Americans still completely divided over the election results of 2016, is a sign that the chaos and division the Russians created is working rather well.

Back in the 2012 election, then presidential candidate Mitt Romney had touted Russia as the "greatest geopolitical threat" to the United States during a debate with President Obama. Rather than acknowledging the real threat Russia posed, Obama offered his own glib assessment.

Obama grinned and joked that "The 1980's were calling to ask for their foreign policy back. Because the Cold War's been over for 20 years." In other words, Obama tried to paint Romney as being behind the times in his assertion that Russia was a major threat.

Perhaps most memorably however was a short time later when former Democratic Senator John Kerry brought the matter up again. Onstage in front of an army of Democratic supporters, Kerry had quipped, "Sarah Palin said she could see Russia from Alaska; Mitt Romney talks like he's only seen Russia by watching Rocky IV!"

Kerry's words soon went viral. And almost immediately droves of witty liberals ran to their social media echo chambers and began collectively raving about how amusing all of this was, while posting sarcastic messages and memes all over Facebook as well as the whole entire twitter-verse. "*OMG! Romney thinks Russia is a threat? That's ridiculous!*"

But my how prescient Mr. Romney has proven himself to be. So much so that former Secretary of State Madeline Albright, who vigorously stumped for President Obama in 2012, actually apologized to Mitt Romney in 2019. In doing so she stated that she and others had greatly "underestimated Russia" at the time.

Whether we view Russia as a threat or not, the Russian government most certainly views the United States as a threat, at least to its national ambition. And as such, certain factions continue to make the disruption of the U.S. and U.S. foreign policy their top priority.

Because the truth is, no matter what some on the Liberal Left and in the mainstream media may think, the real goal of Russian intelligence operations is NOT to support Trump or any other president or presidential candidate. The true goal of the Russians is to create as much polarization and distrust among Americans as they possibly can.

And the fact that we are presently at each other's throats politically is proof that their campaign was indeed highly successful. What many on the Left and the media fail to report when it comes to the Russia Probe is the fact that Mueller's efforts uncovered the real Russian attack on America. And it apparently didn't have anything to do with Donald Trump!

It was all hatched from the Russian intelligence bureau's so-called "Russian Internet Research Agency"—or as it is otherwise less fondly called, "The Troll Farm." Yes, as scary as it is, it seems the Russian federation has weaponized a crack group of internet trolls to use against us.

During the 2016 presidential election, these professional Russian trolls made incendiary social media posts night and day; all in an effort to make different factions of American society despise each other even more than they already did. In fact, according to recent polls, the political/social divide between Americans is presently at an all-time high. Therefore, Mr. Putin must be pretty happy right about now.

CHAPTER 1

Politics, Money, and the Media

"We've got to put a lot of money into changing behavior."
–Bill Gates

IN SOME SENSE, MEDIA has always been on some level beholden to the almighty dollar. Even back in the days when newspapers were the primary form of information and mass communication, every good newsroom editor was always keenly aware that they needed captivating headlines to sell papers and make money.

In this sense, the news is always somewhat geared toward attention getting material that will generate interest and in turn generate revenue. However, what happens when the news is not only passively influenced by prospective everyday consumers, but more so by multimillion dollar corporations and overt agendas of special interest groups? Let's take a look!

The Walt Disney Company currently owns both ESPN and ABC. And Amazon founder Jeff Bezos has basically bought up the Washington Post. Furthermore, Time Warner/AT&T controls CNN, and Comcast runs NBC Universal. Could it be possible that any of the rich executives working for any of these lucrative enterprises would have any interest in influencing the way the news is portrayed?

The answer to that question is of course an emphatic YES, and the facts speak for themselves. Just take for example the story of ABC being under fire when it finally came to light that they were suppressing a story about Disney hiring violent ex-felons as part of their security detail.

Most egregious was the fact that known sexual predators were being selected to oversee the "safety of children" at the busy theme park. Normally such an explosive bombshell would be a headline-generating topic, but not wishing to anger their own corporate taskmasters, ABC kept the story quiet.

It wasn't actually until other news outlets reported the story that it became clear ABC was avoiding any coverage of the situation altogether. But this is just the tip of the iceberg! Folks in the ABC newsroom fretting over whether or not to report stories that make their corporate backers look bad is most certainly not an isolated incident.

Back around the same time ABC was suppressing stories of pedophiles running amuck in Disney World, the network also had one of its own star reporters, Bob Zelnick, resign over a book he wrote which was unfavorable to Al Gore. It was prior to the 2000 presidential election, and left-leaning news executives apparently didn't want to endanger Al Gore's chances of besting George W. Bush for the presidency

As we all know, George Bush Jr. went on to become president anyway. But the fact that ABC would go out of its way to prevent even the mere mention of unflattering remarks about a Democratic presidential candidate, speaks volumes.

And if major news networks carried a liberal bias back then, one can only wonder how oppressive things may be now. Well, as recently as the summer of 2019, it was revealed that a total of 12 NBC/Comcast executives had been heavy donors to the campaign of then Democratic presidential candidate, Kamala Harris.

As well as this influx of cash from the news network, Kamala Harris seemed to have been getting an additional boost from NBC early on in the form of highly favorable coverage. During the first couple of debates she was portrayed as a "breakout star" among the Democratic pack, and her attacks on Joe Biden were hailed as particularly brilliant.

So, she was getting big financial contributions from NBC executives and coincidentally the stories produced by NBC were quite flattering to her campaign. In the case of Kamala, it's not really a matter of pay-for-play, seeing as though she apparently received both *pay and play*!

Knowing that she had been bankrolled by certain networks, it does strike one as rather strange that Kamala went on to eventually drop out of the race citing fundraising as a reason. Taking a swipe at the late entry yet affluent campaigns of Tom Steyer and Michael Bloomberg, she complained that her resources couldn't keep up with the "billionaire" candidates.

News networks and major conflict of interest actually made its way to one of the 2020 Democratic debates, when questions about Net Neutrality were fielded by CNN anchors. Interestingly and ironically, CNN's parent company AT&T has been working overtime to battle Net Neutrality!

Net Neutrality of course, is the concept that internet providers stay neutral when it comes to the kind of content they help to facilitate for consumers. For most of the internet's history it has been neutral and open to the public. However, some parts of the world such as China actively censor the internet service that their citizens receive, but this is the exception and not the norm, at least for now anyway.

Having said that, some sectors of U.S. government have become increasingly concerned that major internet providers could begin to abuse the system, controlling everything from content to internet speeds on a whim. It was for this reason that the Obama administration placed new regulations on providers in 2015, allegedly in an effort to "ensure" net neutrality.

This is where the argument gets a little bit confusing. Because according to internet providers and some proponents of net neutrality itself, the government mandated oversight enacted by the Obama administration (which goes under the heading of "Net Neutrality") actually has the opposite effect of its stated goal.

And rather than helping to ensure net neutrality, according to them the Obama-era regulations instead greatly hamper net neutrality. How is this, you might ask? Because in the government's efforts to step in and arbitrarily play policeman on the Internet, (supposedly to make sure that all content gets a fair shake) it's then suddenly the federal government that becomes the ham-fisted bogeyman forcibly controlling the Internet.

Ajit Pai, who is currently the Chairman for the FCC, once referred to Obama's efforts as simply the government creating a "problem that doesn't exist" in the first place. So, even though the Obama administration put regulations in place under the guise of "Net Neutrality", many like Pai believed that they weren't necessary and might even do more harm than good.

So as strange as it may sound—at least from this perspective—the idea of *repealing the net neutrality laws* put in place by the outgoing Obama administration is seen as actually helping to ensure a very real sense of neutrality free from governmental oversight. According to Pai, rather than bringing neutrality, the Obama-era legislation granted "the power to micromanage virtually every aspect of how the Internet works" to a government agency.

Since the latest Democratic President, Barack Obama championed net neutrality regulations, you would think that the 2020 crop of candidates for the Democratic primary would include the issue at the top of their own agenda, or at the very least make it one of the major talking points in their run for president. Just about every other Obama-era regulation that Trump has rolled back or somehow curtailed is being discussed—so why not Obama's net neutrality regulations?

But there is a curious silence on this issue, and this silence is perhaps the most deafening whenever CNN hosts a Democratic debate. Many believe that this is due to the fact that AT&T owns CNN. So, there you have it folks! Although bringing back net neutrality regulations should be an active part of the Democratic platform, even the Dems can't force CNN (the red headed step child of AT&T) to allow its moderators to bring it up!

But at any rate, beyond the big corporations that fund the media outlets they have acquisitioned, even supposed public corporations like PBS can fall prey to mega donors. Bill Gates for example is a big funder for PBS. This then begs the question—does all of this funding in return bring him friendly coverage for the initiatives of the Gates Foundation? The answer is an absolute YES.

There is a reason why PBS NewsHour does lengthy segments on poverty and AIDS in the developing world, when the mainstream media would rather focus on Donald Trump's latest tweet. It's because of heavy donations from the Bill and Melinda Gates foundation that PBS provides widespread coverage of the group's philanthropist efforts.

One might wonder why covering efforts to help the impoverished of the third world would be a bad thing? It's not. The point is, even if it's for a good cause, stations such as PBS are obviously influenced by those who bankroll them, and their content clearly reflects that fact.

Let's say if some day in the future, Bill Gates or one of his heirs does something that isn't quite so commendable. Considering this glaring conflict of interest, who knows if the story would ever see the light of day? Gates could one day go rogue and viewers of PBS NewsHour wouldn't even know it!

Also, if the Gates foundation ever shifted from paying the media to speak about river blindness in Tanzania, to financing direct discussion of specific political subjects or figures, we would once again be witnessing the classic pay-for-play narrative at work.

The idea of how much of the new content produced by the news media is controlled by their financers is a lively debate and it isn't likely to go away any time soon. Donald Trump of course can be credited with popularizing the phrase "fake news" in his condemnation of the mainstream media, but he isn't the only famous politician to cry foul at the media.

In the summer of 2019, Bernie Sanders was blasted by the Washington Post for insinuating that the Post's owner, Jeff Bezos, was refusing to permit articles that were favorable toward him to appear in the publication.

The topic came up at a campaign stop in New Hampshire, where Bernie was asked what he thought about Amazon not paying taxes in the previous year. Sanders of course is a champion of breaking up billionaire corporations and making them pay their fair share, so this was certainly a subject he couldn't resist.

Sanders grimaced and responded, "I talk about that all of the time. And then I wonder why the Washington Post, which is owned by Jeff Bezos, who owns Amazon, doesn't write particularly good articles about me? I don't know why. But I guess maybe there's a connection. Maybe we helped raise the minimum wage at Amazon to 15 bucks an hour."

The Washington Post of course denies any such thing. And like clockwork, after Bernie's words were launched into the stratosphere and far reaches of cyberspace, the executive editor of the Washington Post, Marty Baron was unleashed on Bernie like an attack dog.

And he did one of the most convenient things that you can do when someone declares something you don't agree with—label them a conspiracy theorist. Baron stated, "Contrary to the conspiracy theory the senator seems to favor, Jeff Bezos allows our newsroom to operate with full independence, as our reporters and editors can attest."

Baron probably didn't see the knowing smile form across Bernie's face when he heard that response. The prompt personal attack on their detractor and the rush to defend their paymaster only plays into the narrative that modern media harbors major conflicts of interest. But unfortunately, this is all just part and parcel to how the news just got bought!

CHAPTER 2

Cultivating the Culture Wars

"As the culture war is about irreconcilable beliefs about God and man, right and wrong, good and evil—and is at root a religious war; it will be with us so long as men are free to act on their beliefs."
—Pat Buchanan

IN AN EXTREMELY DIVERSE country such as the United States there are unfortunately always going to be culture wars of one kind or another, but in recent years we have seen things ratchet up considerably. I myself am old enough to remember a time when an individual's personal political views didn't necessarily define them as a person.

Back in 2004, on a personal level, no one really cared if you voted for George W. Bush or John Kerry. Whether someone liked Bush or someone liked Kerry, it didn't matter too much, and it most likely didn't make you disassociate with or disown them, it simply meant that they had a different opinion.

But my how things have changed! A poll conducted back in 2017, just a few months after Trump was elected, found that 47% of those who identified as Democrats would be "uncomfortable" if they discovered that one of their friends were a Trump supporter.

It used to be that while someone may despise a politician, that rancor usually did not extend to the average person who supported them.

But as the culture wars heat-up, these things have become seemingly fused together, and now if one views a political figure with disdain, it's quite common to view their supporters (or as Hillary might say, their "basketful of deplorables") with an equal measure of animosity.

Diametrically opposed views over certain issues with a complete unwillingness to change by the actors involved has undoubtedly helped stoke the coals of these passionate fires. The easiest example to point out in the current culture wars being waged is the battle between proponents of religious freedom and supporters of the LGBT community.

And before I delve any further into this contentious topic, let me make it absolutely clear that in writing this, I am not attempting to support either side of this culture war, I'm just attempting to present the facts of the conflict as they have transpired. OK—with that albatross discarded off my back, let me begin!

In order to examine the roots of the LGBT/Christian conservative divide, all one has to do is take a look at the Bible. Christians have been taught for over 2000 years that marriage is between one man and one woman. Moreover, homosexuality is also believed by most Christian adherents to be roundly criticized in biblical scripture, from the Old Testament to the New Testament.

I suppose it would be difficult for any devout Christian to disregard these teachings and choose to ignore them. Then again, from the perspective of most LGBT activists, being gay isn't a choice either—it's just the way they are hardwired to be and nothing in the world is really going to change that. So, with such diametrically opposed views seemingly ingrained from birth, cultural conflict is basically all but inevitable.

And since the legalization of gay marriage we have seen several fights play out in public, over seemingly the most trivial of issues. Every couple wants a wedding cake at their wedding, right? A simple enough thing to request and to receive? Well, when you have an LGBT couple request a wedding cake from a devout Christian, it can apparently create an unsavory situation!.

Let's say a Christian baker attempts to explain as politely as possible, "I'm terribly sorry but baking a cake for such an occasion would go against one of the tenants of my deeply held religious beliefs. But I'll gladly recommend you to a secular bake shop just down the street."

Even with these kid gloves on, it would still feel like an insulting and painful slap in the face for the couple being denied the cake. But what can you do? Can you grab a baker's hand and physically force them to bake you a wedding cake? That would be absurd, right? Well herein lies the dilemma. An emotionally charged debate that has already been taken up with the Supreme Court.

During the summer of 2018, in the case of "Masterpiece Cakeshop vs. Colorado Civil Rights Commission", the highest court in the land ruled that the Colorado Civil Rights Commission had been unnecessarily hostile to a Christian-owned cake shop (Masterpiece Cakeshop), by applying incendiary language in their rulings.

In fact, official documentation of the Colorado commission had the cake shop's decision to decline to make a cake for the gay couple, being made comparable to supporting slavery and the holocaust. Yes, baked cakes, icing and all were being equated with the biggest tragedies in human history!

Supreme Court Justice Kennedy noted that such tactics were "inappropriate for a Commission charged with the solemn responsibility of fair and neutral enforcement of Colorado's anti-discrimination law." No matter how you feel about the issue, such language is only adding fuel to the fire.

But casting one simple incident such as this (an issue over who should bake a wedding cake) in such extreme and dire terms is standard procedure for those that wish to rile up and exacerbate the current culture wars our nation is gripped in. These are the kind of people who are quick to dig up the darkest of psychological traumas and use them as ammunition on any given issue.

The Supreme Court, while not directly siding with the bakeshop, made clear their determination that the lower courts not only failed to find an equitable solution for both parties, but they served to make a bad situation even worse. The Supreme Court essentially ruled that the commission was wrongfully targeting and punishing the baker expressly *because of his religious beliefs.*

This raises a point that a few have mentioned before when it comes to the perception that Christians in particular are unfairly targeted in this current spate of culture wars. It has been alleged that while Christians are being subjected to a huge backlash for their beliefs when it comes to same sex marriage, the political left has been conveniently silent when it comes to Muslims and other religious groups.

Islam after all condemns homosexuality just as much, if not more so than Christians. In fact, some Islamic countries still impose the death penalty on people simply accused of engaging in homosexual intercourse. These extreme measures are derived from the Islamic hadith and dictated strictly by Sharia Law.

Considering such an obvious conflict with LGBT, Muslim Americans who also tend to identify with the Democratic Party would seem to be strange bedfellows. But oddly (and perhaps even purposefully) the media is usually rather quiet about this area of conflict in the current culture wars that we face.

Even in 2016 when a panel representing 51 Islamic nations dramatically petitioned the U.N. to keep LGBT activists from taking part in the "2016 High Level Meeting on Ending Aids", it barely made news in the West. You also don't hear too much about traditional Islamic bakeries being taken to court by LGBT couples.

Although, as the investigative journalism piece conducted by conservative activist Steven Crowder in 2015 revealed—Islamic bakers are in just as much of a quandary as Christian bakers. Crowder and an associate posing as a gay couple, took to the streets in the Muslim enclave of Dearborn, Michigan on a mission to get a wedding cake.

What was the result? They were roundly rejected at just about every Muslim cakes shop and bakery they entered. Yet, no one seems eager to hold Islam to the same scrutinizing standard as Christianity. For whatever reason, it's primarily Christians who seem to be on the frontline in this particular fight.

And although we are just now seeing these sorts of things being played out in such spectacular fashion in the courts, the conflict between religious freedom and LGBT groups has had the potential to erupt for decades. It basically wasn't until political parties on both sides felt it was expedient to weaponize the issue and make it a major part of their polarizing platforms, that it became front and center in the culture wars.

It was back in the 2012 election that two completely different polarizing lines were drawn in the sand. For it was that year that you had both the Republican and Democratic candidate weaponizing the concept of marriage for the benefit of their respective base.

On one side Mitt Romney was declaring his firm belief that "marriage is between one man and one woman" and on the other President Barack Obama was steadfastly proclaiming that people should have the right to love and marry anyone they so choose.

The election of course resulted in President Obama receiving another term and gay marriage becoming the law of the land. Since then, Democrats have been seen as the pro-LGBT party, whereas the Republicans, who have a long track record of either stifling or outright opposing progressive LGBT legislation, are perceived as the great opponents to LGBT issues.

The Republicans are also usually viewed as the defenders of the faith when it comes to the rights of conservative religious groups. These polarized positions in the current culture wars seem relatively fixed in place. Though some would argue that Donald Trump presents a bit of a wild card in the conflict.

Because while Trump is a strong supporter of religious conservatives and so-called religious freedom, he has also voiced his support of LGBT. Unlike Vice President Mike Pence, Trump is actually quite friendly (at least on the surface) with the LGBT community.

In reality, Trump would want nothing more than to capture some of the Democrat's LGBT support, making him perhaps the first Republican president to seek the LGBT vote. Legislation wise however, he is mainly viewed by most LGBT activists as going against their agenda.

Although Trump has been recognized as an advocate for greater rights of the LGBT community overseas and has appointed openly gay officials in his cabinet, he has also curtailed transgender legislation. Most notably, the Trump administration placed restrictions on transgender soldiers in the U.S. military.

Trump is also responsible for the nomination of two very conservative Supreme Court justices, who lean more toward religious freedom than they ever would LGBT rights. Nevertheless, Trump does remain the most openly supportive Republican president to date when it comes to LGBT issues as a whole.

After all, Trump was the one that had the openly gay co-founder of PayPal, Peter Thiel, stand up at the RNC convention in 2016 and proclaim that he was "gay, a Republican, and an American" to thunderous applause. Such things would have been unheard of in previous Republican campaigns.

But again, with the exception of the slightly ambitious approach of Donald Trump, the two camps still seem by and large, diametrically opposed. It is a situation that has the potential for volatile friction between supporters of opposing parties.

With such extremes, someone who claims to be a Republican is typically not going to be viewed very favorably by a Democratic LGBT supporter. This volatility of the culture wars trickles down into just about every aspect of society. Just think about how intensely heated things have become.

If a conservative, Republican supporter is seated in a work cubicle next to a liberal, Democratic LGBT supporter, just how well might they get along? Some who have a sense of humor and fairness, or the ability to look beyond intrinsic ideology might fare all right. However, all too often there will be a 'situation' in the works since the differing ideologies are drawn up and viewed in such extreme terms.

From the perspective of the LGBT supporter, a Republican in their midst is not just someone who disagrees with them, as the stakes have been set much higher than that. Things are so polarized that the other side is perceived to be not only against their politics, but also against them as a person.

Politics you see, have not only become polarized, they have become painfully *personalized* in ways that they never were in the past. Now, someone on the other side of the aisle isn't just someone with a differing point of view, they're seen as the antagonist who is threatening their very way of life by virtue of their beliefs.

Having that said, as soon as a liberal LGBT supporter in the workplace looks over and sees a Trump/Pence sticker plastered on the cubicle wall next to them, you just know that there is a possibility for a problem. At the very least there will likely be plenty of awkward moments and cold looks in that breakroom.

Not only that, due to this current culture war there are substantial conflicts being waged over the very core principals of certain employers. For instance, if a Christian based school or organization hires an employee whose lifestyle goes against the tenants of the institution's beliefs as presented in their charter, this is yet another recipe for an unsavory situation.

Just take the example of what happened with Roncalli High School, which is a Catholic-based school located in Indianapolis, Indiana. The school has a long history and tradition that prides itself on deeply-held religious beliefs that are of course conservative, yet it is located in one of the most progressive and liberal parts of the city.

For the most part, this never really constituted much of a problem, but when it was discovered that one of the female guidance counselors at the school had married another woman, the school was suddenly (though not surprisingly) in an all-out crisis. The counselor, Shelley Fitzgerald, was very popular with both students and staff and no one really wanted to see her go.

Regardless, right there in the school's charter and on each and every job application anyone submits to be hired as a staff member, it states that the school's religious belief is that marriage is between one man and one woman. It then makes it clear that to be considered for employment the applicant must confirm that they agree with that belief.

The teacher in question had to have seen that detail in the job application, and also must have specified she agreed with the school's position on marriage. Yet somewhere along the way she ended up in a same-sex marriage. Now the Christian based school had to figure out how to address this new sticky situation they found themselves in.

No matter how you might feel about same-sex marriage, just try to see it from the school's perspective for a moment. As this scandal unfolded, the school was presented with a fairly stark choice. Either they allow the teacher to stay on and completely rewrite their cherished charter, or they fire her for violating that said charter. These were really the only two options that Roncalli really had!.

Then again, try to put yourself in the shoes of Shelley Fitzgerald. From her perspective she was just trying to do her job when her personal life came under fire. It's a difficult situation either way you look at it. This is the problem when a political party becomes tied to the very identity or the core beliefs of a person.

When this occurs, any criticism of either party or even having an alternative view is perceived as a personal attack on the other side. It's hard to get two different groups to "agree to disagree" when they feel that the other side of the spectrum is wishing to either tear down their personal beliefs or disrespect who they are as a person.

And until either Christians begin to deny some of their core principles, or LGBT groups learn to ignore the beliefs of Christians—one can only expect these increasingly volatile culture wars to continue in full force.

Hillary Clinton waded knee-deep into this culture war in 2016, siding heavily with members of the LGBT community. For it was this year that she went on the record to state that the Christian views "have to be changed." If Clinton won the 2016 election perhaps she would have made good on her suggestion, and somehow attempted to forcibly coerce religious groups to change their beliefs for her beliefs.

As of the writing of this book however, religious freedom is still a valued and secure part of our society, just as much as inclusion and equal rights for our fellow LGBT Americans. So it seems that this conflict will unfortunately continue for the unforeseeable future.

This is of course not the only example of culture wars run amuck. Issues over race, immigration, abortion, and state's rights (just to name a few) still cause plenty of friction, but the culture war revolving around religious freedom and LGBT activists is the one that is currently front and center.

CHAPTER 3

Quantifying the Value of the Vote

"Politics—I still think it's a bunch of liars and a bunch of self-interest. It's not about the people; it's about themselves and their rise to power. They are voting on things based on whether they will have the support of the people when they vote next time. They [politicians] don't have the balls to say, 'I believe in this! I don't care what happens [come election time]!"

–Jay-Z (AKA Shawn Carter)

A CLASSIC MISNOMER OF American government is that the United States is a democracy. While there are most certainly democratic elements present in the process, the U.S. is in reality a republic that utilizes representative-government. The democracy aspect of it comes into play during elections when people cast their votes for the politicians that will end up representing them.

Any lawmaking and future legislative decisions will be carried out by those chosen representatives, and not just some Joe Schmo down the street. However, what is the value of our vote really worth once we elect our representatives & senators and send them off to Washington DC?

Before we get into all that however, let's first take a look at the biggest election in the land; which of course is the presidential. Unlike the midterms, the presidential election is determined by the Electoral College rather than the total number of popular votes. Therefore, in a presidential election there are cases in which certain votes may be significantly less valuable than others. For instance, someone living in the great state of Indiana could very well find themselves in this situation.

This is because with the exception of Indianapolis, some surrounding suburbs, and northern enclaves of Indiana such as Gary and South Bend tend to trend Republican. And if someone here, wished to vote for a Democratic presidential candidate, 9 times out of 10 their vote really wouldn't matter too much anyway.

I know it sounds discouraging, and it's not the sort of thing you would say at a get-out-the-vote rally, but as long as this process continues, it is how it goes. Obama happened to break this pattern in 2008, just barely squeaking a win out of Indiana. And unlike the swing state of Ohio, which frequently goes back and forth on the electoral map, Indiana is not traditionally a battleground state.

In fact, over the past few decades Indiana has quite consistently remained in the red state camp. And when you know that the trend is likely to continue, it may seem a little bit futile casting a vote for the Democratic candidate, when the odds of your state's electoral college are so firmly stacked against your pick.

It is precisely for this reason that some in the Democratic Party have suggested that the Electoral College should be completely abolished. It is true that if the Electoral College ceased to exist, every individual vote would indeed count. If things weren't determined by state electoral colleges, but rather the popular vote on a national level, then even one lone blue vote in a predominantly red state would surely matter more. This is because when counted with all of the other blue votes it would contribute to the total national vote, no matter what state the ballot was cast in.

Another fact not lost on Democrats is that if elections were determined by the sheer volume of popular votes cast rather than how many states were picked up in the Electoral College, Hillary Clinton would have been elected president in 2016.

Because yes, even though Trump won the Electoral College by a decisive margin (304 votes vs. Hillary's 227) Clinton actually bested Trump in the popular vote by nearly 3 million votes. Her total vote count at the end of the day was 65,853,514, whereas Trump's came in at 62,984,828.

But the founding fathers of this nation came up with the Electoral College for a reason. The idea of using this process rather than counting each individual vote was implemented in order to better ensure that the entirety of the United States was fully represented. This way, with the Electoral College vote spread out across the nation, small states with lower populations would not be completely overshadowed by big states with larger populations.

To be sure, larger states such as California, Texas, New York, and Florida have the largest electoral votes attached to them with 55, 36, and 29 respectively. But all the same, plenty of states that carry between 10 and 20 votes are still prized points of conquest for presidential candidates.

Since candidates need to piece together an electoral majority (of at least 270) by way of a coalition of several states, it forces politicians to campaign and focus on a wide variety of electorate locales. If victory was based on just the popular vote however, candidates might be more inclined to simply touch down in party strongholds with heavy populations, such as the aforementioned states of California, Texas, New York, and Florida.

This would then essentially make these heavily populated states the true king makers, while the disenfranchised folks across the rest of America would feel as if their votes mattered very little. Then again, it is the very Electoral College system that creates the idea of "Battle Ground States", which both candidates in an election aim to swing in their direction.

For example, Ohio is seen as a swing state and therefore is always vigorously fought for and campaigned in. But deeply entrenched states such as California (which almost always goes to the Democratic party) and Texas (which almost always goes to Republicans) barely get a mention by the presidential candidates.

Since they know that these certain states are basically a "sure thing" for their respective parties, they wisely determine that their efforts and resources would be better spent elsewhere. This at the same time creates some level of disenfranchisement for both those who would vote contrary and those who support the standard, since they do not receive as much attention from either of the main candidates in a national election.

Nevertheless, the Electoral College has its clear advantages. It's this system after all that prevents a third party from getting to power by gleaning merely a fraction of the vote. Hypothetically speaking, if someday there were a popular third-party candidate, without the Electoral College in place, that candidate could possibly win the presidency with just about one-third of the vote.

This would mean that we would have someone elected to the highest office of the land with only 33% of the vote. This would leave a whopping two-thirds of the electorate who did not vote for this particular candidate feeling decidedly disenfranchised as a result.

Just think about it, things are polarized enough when half of the country doesn't like who's elected, but when a full two-thirds don't like and/or didn't vote for the president? That's basically a recipe for discontentment and disaster! The Electoral College actually safeguards against this, because even a third-party candidate would still have to win a solid majority of the states in the Electoral College before they advanced to the White House.

Now that we've discussed the impact of the Electoral College on presidential elections; let's go over what's at stake during a midterm election. During the midterms when voters cast their ballot for representatives and senators who are up for re-election, it's done by direct ballot. That means that there is no Electoral College involved, and this way it really is just a matter of who gets the most votes.

This is precisely why the midterms have so many narrow matchups that it can sometimes take weeks to tally the votes and determine the winner. In such an election there is no question that your input as a voter is important, because in this case literally every single vote counts.

Take for example the 2008 election of Alaska's former Republican representative Mike Kelly. It was indeed a close race, and in the end when all the votes were counted, Mike defeated his opponent by literally one single vote! So, if you lived in Mike's district in Alaska and were dead set on voting for his opponent that election day but chose to sleep in instead, it could very well be your fault that Mike got re-elected! This is proof that every vote really does count in a midterm election

So, after going over all of the issues presented in this chapter—are your votes worth it? The answer is yes, but the impact of each vote depends on all of the factors we've gone over. And when it comes to the presidential elections in particular, while the Electoral College may be an imperfect system, it is still the best one that we have for now, and removing it would likely make matters worse or at least more unpredictable than they already are.

CHAPTER 4

The Establishment of the Elite

"Voting is completely important. People in America think democracy is a given. I think of it as an ecosystem, and what gets in the way of it is politicians and apathy."
—Henry Rollins

THEY LIVE IN THE wealthiest well-secured communities on the East and West Coasts, and jet across America in the luxury of their first-class seats, never giving much consideration to the concerns and living conditions of those struggling down below. It almost sounds like some kind of dystopian nightmare, but this scenario is all too real in American society.

From dogma preaching elitist professors locked away in their ivory towers, to Lori Laughlin using her fame and fortune to literally buy her daughter's way into a prestigious, Ivy League school, the dollar induced disconnect between the elite (also known as the 1%) and the rest of us has grown exponentially over the past few decades.

Some have cited Hillary Clinton's failure of capturing the White House in 2016 as being partly due to her perceived disconnect with the working class. Trump on the other hand portrayed himself as the champion of working-class values despite the fact that he's always been wealthy.

He trumpeted for all to hear that he was the candidate who would take on business as usual and bring the jobs back. Many have wondered how a billionaire from New York could become so relatable to say, poor blue-collar workers in Ohio—but the way Trump framed his argument was actually kind of convincing.

He blamed wasteful regulation and inept management for the low pay and loss of jobs in places like the Midwest. He then presented a plan as to how he would bring those jobs back, and this became a major pillar of his campaign. Even if not all of his pledges were upheld, he at least had a plan. He had something to say that caught the attention of working-class voters, and many attentively listened.

Hillary Clinton on the other hand barely developed a rapport with the working class at all. In the aftermath of the 2016 election, some have begun to postulate that liberal Democrats like Hillary have themselves become part of a new class of elitists, completely blind to the concerns and conditions of the less affluent citizenry.

Is there any truth in this? According to Tucker Carlson, a conservative journalist and Fox News personality; the answer is an absolute "yes!". I know some of you who are reading this might be turned off by Fox News, but let's just take a look at his argument, because in many ways it is quite convincing.

Tucker views the current state of affairs in America as something akin to an "Oligarchy" posing as a democracy. Interestingly enough, this is actually an argument that is also echoed by far-left liberals. All one has to do is look at Bernie Sanders, who constantly proclaims that America is becoming an oligarchy controlled by the billionaire class.

According to Tucker, it was this powerful oligarchy that found themselves absolutely dumbfounded at the results of the 2016 election. Tucker maintains that Hillary was the chosen candidate of the political elite. It is evidenced that she was preordained, given the fact that she was paired up against a field of somewhat weaker, and more obscure candidates during the Democratic primary.

Tucker also points out that in 2016, Trump was not only disliked by the Democratic establishment, but also widely attacked by the Republican establishment as well. Trump was never approved by the mainstream Republican political machine, being viewed as far too risky to hedge any bets on.

Given a choice, the top mainstream candidate probably would have been George W. Bush's younger brother Jeb Bush. But when it became clear early-on that Jeb wasn't going to win, the elites focused on supporting the next "rational" candidate. Well, Trump trounced all of these rational candidates one after the other, until eventually the only one the establishment could root for was Texas Senator, Ted Cruz.

However, Ted Cruz was not very popular with the Republican establishment either, and many high-ranking Republicans severely disliked him. Yet, he was viewed as a relatively safe bet when compared to the wild card that Trump represented. And in the final weeks that led up to Trump's nomination, when the only Republican candidates left on the field were Trump, Cruz, and Ohio Governor John Kasich, national television was rife with "Stop Trump" adds funded by Republicans!

These advertisements would bluntly instruct Republicans to vote for Ted Cruz, because "Kasich can't do it. The math won't work." This was in reference to the impossibility of John Kasich obtaining enough delegates to gain the nomination during the last stretch of the Republican primary.

In the fevered desperation of these Republicans to stop Trump in the final days, there was even the laughable so-called "collusion" attempt between Ted Cruz and John Kasich. In this last attempt to grasp at straws, Kasich and Cruz agreed to focus their efforts in specific states that they were most favored to win. Kasich agreed to focus on Ohio for example, while basically ceding his efforts in Indiana over to Cruz. An arrangement Kasich later denied though Cruz still tacitly supported.

It was only when Trump decisively defeated Cruz and masses of Trump supporters protested at the RNC's delay in nominating Trump, that the Republican leadership had to finally admit Trump as their nominee. Many forget the fact that the status quo of the RNC (or the ruling class if you will) was just about as hesitant, if not more so than the Democratic elite when it came to accepting Trump.

The fact that his own party begrudgingly accepted him has made Trump and his supporters rightfully suspicious of what he calls the "Swamp" in Washington DC. Making some wonder if this entrenched ruling class has been trying to actively thwart the president and his policies at every turn ever since he took office.

And now that Trump has been impeached by the House of Representatives in Congress, many are wondering if the ruling elite are actually trying to actively overturn the will of the American people who cast their votes in 2016. Tucker Carlson describes the ability of democracies to cast votes as a much needed "pressure-relief valve" that keeps the inflamed passion of society "from exploding."

In other countries when the majority of citizens become infuriated with the ruling class, they often stage a revolt, but in America we go to the ballot box. Though if Trump is officially impeached and then removed from office on seemingly meritless grounds that even the least politically savvy members of the American electorate can see through, then the ruling elite have essentially ignored and closed-off this essential societal pressure valve. When this sort of societal pressure builds, who knows what might happen as a result?

If citizens can no longer trust that their input at the ballot box means anything, they will no longer look toward votes to create change in government and society. Instead, the disaffected voter whose votes were so callously nullified by a greedy, self-serving elite just might take other measures. The outcome of such a revolt is too troubling to even elaborate on, but it does seem to constitute a disturbing and frightening possibility if establishment politicians finally go too far.

So, just who are these elites that seem so blind to and detached from the dangerous environment they are helping to create? Whether liberal left or far right conservative, the elitists typically have a few things in common. They are those that have passed (or in some cases bought) the SAT's with flying colors, and then went on to a prestigious university that only a select few attend such as Harvard or Yale.

Author and political commentator Nassim Taleb, has a rather interesting term to describe this elite, cream of the crop. He calls them "Intellectual Yet Idiot" or "IYI" for short. As much as this might sound like a put-down or snarky remark, as Nassim points out, in many ways it really is an apt description.

Because as Nassim sees it, most of these Ivy League scholars are highly intellectual when it comes to writing about political theory and crafting academic treatises. Yet whenever they are forced to apply themselves to real world problems, they quickly prove themselves to be inept, out of depth, and completely idiotic in their actions.

Nassim has called out this 'out of touch' political elite. He asserts that these budding elitists are the kind of people who hopped through all the hurdles required at their prestigious universities with flying colors. They hobnobbed and kissed-up to their Ivy League professors who in turn wrote "glowing letters of recommendation" to governmental gatekeepers of the bureaucracy.

These senior bureaucrats then gladly open the door for the idiotic elite, so that they can sit on government backed boards and panels indefinitely while happily dispelling their inept doctrines that have no real meaning in the real world.

With their profession in the bureaucracy ensured, they then move on to an equally prestigious community; preferably on the East or West Coast. The next strategic move is to wed someone with a similar wealthy background. These folks then take up high-level managerial, professional, and political positions, which allow them to further perpetuate their standing among the elite class.

Many of these people quickly acquire vast wealth that propels them up to the legendary 1% status of the elite. This is the likes of which Bernie Sanders continually speaks out about; leaving all other segments of American society in their prestigious and well-refined dust. Another element of this burgeoning elite is not so much bureaucratic as it is liberal technocrat.

It used to be that the liberal left was against big corporations, but by the late 1990's with the rise of the Silicon Valley and certain whiz kids such as Chad Hurley, Steve Chen, Jawed Karim, Mark Zuckerberg, Steve Jobs, Bill Gates, Larry Page and Sergey Brin (not to mention auxiliary add-ons such as Jeff Bezos and Elon Musk) Some Democrats were suddenly all about the same corporate excess that supposedly only Republicans dream of and pursue.

And coincidentally enough, almost all of the aforementioned individuals are in the Democratic orbit, or at least left leaning and liberal in many of their sentiments. Even so, when any given Democratic actor strains their leash and goes a little bit too far, even these elite left leaning technocrats of the top 1% are provoked to say something.

When Elizabeth Warren recently said that she planned to establish a wealth tax on the wealthiest Americans, this prompted even the infamously shy Bill Gates to complain about it. He told news media in response to this proclamation that he doesn't mind giving "his fair share" to charities. "But when you say I should pay $100 billion, that's something else entirely." Elizabeth Warren, seemingly chastised, then made some conciliatory, almost apologetic remarks in which she walked back much of her previous rhetoric.

Democrats also used to be on the side of labor unions when they held strikes and protests against the big factories and warehouses. But nowadays they are more likely to be on the side of billionaire Jeff Bezos, the ideologically liberal owner of Amazon, a company that boasts the most prolific series of workhouses the world has ever known. And don't forget, Bezos also owns the Washington Post, which is one of the most strident critics of President Donald Trump.

This of course only endears the likes of Bezos to the elite Democratic leadership even more. And the same goes for Apple, whose offshore factories in China have Chinese workers laboring to assemble the world's smartphones for just a couple bucks each. Although, since Apple is firmly planted within the liberal wing of the elite, no one says one word about it.

Not too long ago, liberal activists would have been in the streets protesting the corporate greed of such companies, but now it's just business as usual and seems to be accepted. Nor do they have to be troubled by China's crackdown on the quasi-democratic denizens of Hong Kong, for as long as the money and status quo continue, the elite leadership is just fine.

But every once in a while, an outspoken individual seems to ruffle the elite's feathers. Donald Trump is certainly one of those, and he's definitely not the only one. Because during the 2020 Democratic primaries, even Trump couldn't seem to enrage the liberal elite as much as a controversial congresswoman from Hawaii named Tulsi Gabbard did.

She began to openly question the Democratic taskmasters of the DNC during her campaign. She also questioned some key democratic talking points such as how to deal with immigration. For this she received immediate blowback and soon enough none other than former presidential candidate, Hillary Clinton, was weighing in.

Strangely, the woman who brought us rumors of a "vast right-wing conspiracy" in the late 1990's when Bill Clinton was impeached was once again talking conspiracy. On a talk radio show she made the baseless claim that Tulsi Gabbard was a Russian asset.

Tulsi Gabbard immediately fired back, taking up arms with the biggest media weapon of modern times, aka Twitter. She dove right into the twitter-verse and in a fiery post, declared, "Great! Thank you Hillary Clinton. You, the queen of warmongers, embodiment of corruption, and personification of the rot that has sickened the Democratic Party for so long, have finally come out from behind the curtain."

An entirely incensed Gabbard then went on to say, "From the day I announced my candidacy there has been a concerted campaign to destroy my reputation. We wondered who was behind it and why. Now we know—it was always you, through your proxies and powerful allies in the corporate media and war machine, afraid of the threat I pose."

Here we can see that Tulsi clearly believes that the Democratic establishment by way of Hillary and her "proxies and powerful allies" is actively trying to influence the Democratic primary. Just what exactly are the liberal elites afraid of when it comes to a candidate like Tulsi Gabbard?

What they likely fear most is her independent streak and straight talk. Gabbard has proven herself to be a free and independent thinker, one who will not simply toe the party line, especially if she feels that it goes against her beliefs and ethics

This is something she has proven time and time again. Whether it's over the economy, foreign policy, or any other issue, Tulsi stands her ground. Most recently she did so in dramatic fashion by breaking ranks with her party and refusing to vote 'yes' on the 2019 impeachment of Donald Trump; Gabbard simply voted 'present'.

In the hyper-partisan climate of the Democratic Party today, that's enough to be branded a traitor. But Tulsi doesn't care, she's strong-willed and won't be bullied or pushed aside. This is precisely why the elite establishment of the Democratic Party probably fear her so much. For most of them she is entirely too unpredictable and independent to tolerate.

Some have even speculated that she could leave the Democratic Party entirely and run as an Independent. For Democratic elite who fear that such a run could dilute the Democratic vote and end up helping Trump, this could be considered tantamount to high treason. To the established elite wish to keep their ruling order steady, this is a prime threat that will indeed be challenged at every turn.

Tulsi herself recently acknowledged these challenges in a heartfelt message to her supporters, by stating, "If they can falsely portray me as a traitor, then they can do it to anyone. And in fact, that's exactly the message that they want to get across to you. That if you stand up against Hillary and the party power brokers—if you stand up to the rich and powerful elite and the war machine, they will destroy you and discredit your message."

Regardless of the pushback from her own party, Tulsi Gabbard's convictions remain steady as she continues to take on the establishment. In her view there is absolutely no question that an elite establishment exists; but how does one deal with or dismantle it? Well, for starters, Gabbard has recently filed a 50 million dollar lawsuit against Clinton because of her slanderous accusations.

CHAPTER 5

Digging up the Deep State

"The most terrifying words in the English language are—
I'm from the government and I'm here to help."
–President Ronald Reagan

THE DEEP STATE. THE right winger's bogeyman of a supposed overarching system consisting of entrenched government bureaucrats attempting to circumvent the will of the American people and the representatives that they voted into office. Does such an undermining monster actually exist? It seems the answer to that question largely depends on whom you ask!

Many liberals and most of the news media outlets will contest that the Deep State is nothing more than a far-fetched right-wing conspiracy theory. Consequently anyone who dares to even consider its existence as a possibility will likely be looked at as if they've lost their mind. Even so, some would say that not only does the Deep State exist, but that there is a paper trail to backup their belief!

These true believers point to Inspector General Michael E. Horowitz's report in late 2019. The report was regarding the FISA warrants that were issued during the 2016 campaign as evidence of an implicit bias orchestrated by Deep State actors against then candidate Donald Trump.

All of this could very well indicate some nefarious dealings at a deep, bureaucratic level of U.S. government. However, the term "Deep State" itself actually first came into use in reference, to the military industrial complex of Turkey, not the entrenched bureaucracy of the United States.

Turkey? Yes—Turkey. The country that was the seat of the former Islamic powerhouse known as the Ottoman Empire. The Empire fell apart after coming out on the losing side of World War I. From its ashes, remnants of Turkey's military forged a new bastion for pure Turkish nationalism by creating the modern "Republic of Turkey."

Since its inception in the 1920's, throughout the Republic's brief history, military coups have periodically occurred to unseat leaders that have fallen out of favor. In fact, as recently as 2015, a cabal of political agitators and factions of the Turkish military worked together in a failed attempt to take down the Turkish President, Recep Tayyip Erdogan, and he's still in power today.

The Turkish citizenry have called this impulse to undo elections in Turkey a product of the "Deep State." Could the United States own cabal of high-level intelligence operatives, political appointees, and military officials be part of a similar apparatus that's hell-bent on launching a soft coup against the duly elected president of the United States?

This is what many Trump supporters, and on occasion Donald Trump himself, would have you believe. According to them, all of the unelected career bureaucrats that were trotted out before the impeachment hearing in 2019 (from Ambassador Bill Taylor, to Colonel Vindman) were all part and parcel to this deep state apparatus at work.

Some Fox News personalities such as Judge Jeannine Pirro second this opinion, claiming that actors from the murky deep were spreading disruption from the very beginning of Trump's candidacy for president. Pirro claims that these Deep State cronies "worked to spy on and frame a presidential candidate and plant the seed for his overthrow in the ugliest, most corrupt attempted political coup in U.S. History."

Where's the proof? Well, according to Jeannine and those with a similar perspective, it's in the recent report conducted by the Justice Department's IG (Inspector General), Michael E. Horrowitz. This report details the decision behind the execution of the original Russia probe and supposedly, demonstrates the Deep State in action. But how?

Although Horrowitz himself stressed that he "found no intentional misconduct or political bias" on those conducting the investigation, he did find several "significant inaccuracies and omissions" when it came to the criteria utilized for FISA applications.

But Horrowitz would appear to be a lone wolf howling in the deep state wilderness, because Trump's attorney general William Barr, as well as United States Attorney John Durham, both roundly rejected his conclusion, and instead opened up a separate investigation of their own.

William Barr has declared the whole ordeal that kick started all of the Russian collusion accusations was based on the "thinnest of suspicions." And that FISA requests were conducted over what amounted to little more than hearsay, false pretenses, and assumptions.

It seems that the wholesale spying on a presidential campaign was encouraged out of much innuendo and unchecked intrigue. The findings revealed that it was by this means that the FBI used FISA inquiries into staffer Carter Page with the goal of gaining access to "another high-level campaign official who was not a subject of the probe."

In other words, the Deep State dug up Page and other campaign staffers in order to take swipes at Donald Trump. The fact that the IG would claim this was not only a mistake but in fact several mistakes which occurred in a random sort of comedy of errors, is rather hard to believe.

To many, it seems like nothing short of an orchestrated intelligence hit on an American citizen, for no other reason than someone somewhere doesn't like him too much. Is this the divisive Deep State at work? The interesting thing is that Trump suspected he was being spied on by some sort of shadowy intelligence agency and had commented as such during the 2016 campaign.

Yet at the time, most didn't take him seriously, while many

proclaimed him to be paranoid and a conspiracy theorist. If anything else, the IG report proves that Trump was not paranoid; he was actually quite justified in his suspicions. Top-level bureaucrats from deep within the state department were absolutely after him.

Seen under this light, when a government operative like the FBI's Peter Strzok sent a random, offhand text to a colleague during the 2016 election that stated "we're going to stop it" in reference to Trump's successful run for president. The vague "we" that he referred to seems to imply there's a shadowy Deep State group.

Belief in the Deep State is actually bipartisan in nature, and how one views the Deep State unsurprisingly depends on party affiliation. Some Democratic believers have even gone so far as to praise the Deep State. Why would they do that?

Well, once again it depends on perspective. Because for these Democratic ideologues, it is the Trump administration that's the true nefarious threat to the nation, whereas the Deep State made-up of "dedicated government officials" is a kind of "praetorian guard." An essential bureaucratic bulwark that is helping in preventing the country from going off the rails during the "turbulent" Trump presidency.

According to author and former Washington insider Mike Lofgren however, the idea of an American deep state is much more troubling than this simplistic polarized perspective implies. Lofgren contends that ever since the Obama administration, certain low-level bureaucrats have become entrenched in government and have "weaponized federal, state, and local law enforcement" agencies.

Probably the clearest evidence of this was the abuse recently uncovered at the IRS. Many honest taxpayers view the Internal Revenue Service with a bit of dread, but not because they are doing anything wrong. It's simply because of the powerful authority the IRS has over their lives and the consequences of not complying

Under good stewardship the IRS is an agency for the good and the betterment of the nation, but when misdirected and abused, it could most definitely be a major tool of tyranny. Just think of how many lives would be ruined if they were being singled out and targeted by vindictive bureaucrats from the Internal Revenue Service.

Sadly, this one is not just hypothetical, as it's something that really happened. In 2013 the Inspector General for the Tax Administration found that the IRS had been specifically targeting conservative/ Republican nonprofits with punitive reprisals for their "political beliefs." What were these reprisals? They came in the form of audits, additional penalties, and longer delays!

The targeting was done by low level IRS officials who made it a part of their policy to specifically go after taxpayers associated with the Tea Party and other conservative groups. It is said that these groups were labeled as either "Tea Party" or "Patriots" in their official records, which meant they were priority for this unwarranted scrutiny.

These groups were automatically placed on the "BOLO" list. BOLO stands for "Be On the Look Out." And just what were these supposed tax professionals on the lookout for? Was it malfeasance or wrongdoing ? Nope, they were on the lookout for political views not particularly palatable to the Obama administration.

Despite this, after everything was exposed, President Obama himself denied any knowledge of these activities. Obama stated at a press conference that the alleged actions by IRS personnel were "outrageous." He then went on to assure the public that any IRS employee found to be using such discriminatory tactics would be "held accountable".

While that all sounds well and good, as of 2020 there has been virtually zero accountability of these bloated, bureaucratic, political hacks. However, a few apologies have been offered here and there. One in particular was from Lois Lerner, the head of the bureaucratic IRS division that was discovered to be targeting conservatives. She instantly issued an apology upon the outset of the scandal.

When questioned before a panel of the American Bar Association on May 10th, 2013, Lerner stated that both she and the IRS were "apologetic" for what she called, "absolutely inappropriate actions." At the same time Lerner shielded Obama and his inner-circle by claiming that the misdeeds were not ordered from the top, but rather were "done by low-level front-line people."

Just who were these low-level front-line bureaucrats Mrs. Lerner spoke of? Were they perhaps part of the Deep State? If you view the group as a bunch of unelected bureaucrats run amuck, I guess the answer would be yes. But is Lerner telling the truth? Was this just a one-time aberration, or part of a more elaborate plot?

As some have pointed out, perhaps the truth lies somewhere in-between. Maybe it really was just the work of a few isolated agents. This interpretation provides the more sober view, reminding us that all governments have a sort of deep state apparatus within the fixtures, and there is nothing nefarious OR heroic about it.

Because according to this interpretation, at the end of the day it's just a bunch of common, career bureaucrats who either do their job ethically and honestly, or completely corruptly. Either way, they work while the unpredictable winds of political fate continually shift before them.

At any rate, if the Deep State doesn't already exist, it seems more than likely that it will in the near future, as the so-called "resistance" to Trump continues to grow in the opposition's camp. The resistance would by its very nature wish to topple Trump's administration as they continue their quest to teardown the new foundation that he is trying to establish.

CHAPTER 6

The Real Deal OR Fake News?

"When people talk about fake news, you know, a lot of folks just roll their eyes, like 'Oh, you know, whatever; people will figure it out.' [But] the truth is—they don't always figure it out."
–Megyn Kelly

IN THE PAST, FAKE news was something that came to mind when we thought of tabloid magazines heralding headlines about Bigfoot and midnight rides on UFOs. But in recent years the phrase has taken on a meaning far greater than any fabricated feature from the National Enquirer.

American confidence in the competence and integrity of mainstream media outlets is at an all-time low. This means that once respected major news networks like ABC, CBS, NBC, and CNN are now considered untrustworthy by a large portion of the population. Are these newfound doubts justified?

In exploring that question, let's create for ourselves a brief timeline of documented instances in which the mainstream media was caught red-handed in patently peddling false information. The first incident that I would like to remind readers of is the infamous faux pas committed by CBS back in the 2004 presidential election.

That particular election year saw an incumbent Republican

president, George W. Bush facing off against a Democratic challenger, John Kerry. Although none would have thought it then, when compared with today's political environment, those were less polarizing times.

Sure, you had typical partisan hacks on both sides. However, unlike the past few presidential elections, the 2004 election was not presented as some life or death struggle, so much as it was run simply on who was better equipped to lead.

The argument to stay the course with Bush was often due to his integrity as a capable leader. Both Bush and Kerry had served in some capacity in the military, with Kerry famously seeing active duty in the Vietnam War, while Bush had a more comfortable stint at home in the Texas Air National Guard.

Bush's integrity was suddenly called into question when Dan Rather of CBS news aired an unvetted story on the TV program "60 Minutes". He questioned Bush's service in the Air National Guard, or more specifically whether Bush had actually "fulfilled his duties with the guard." And if he had certain strings pulled in order to get him into a relatively safe role within the military.

Without coming right out and saying it, the suggestion was pretty clear. Bush was being accused of being a coward who avoided getting drafted into active duty in Vietnam through the help of his rich and powerful father, who secured him a "safe" position close to home with the Air National Guard.

This seemed to be what Dan Rather was basically suggesting, and in the segment he brought further documents along with a witness that seemed to backup this story. The only trouble is—none of it was true. Rather showed a list of memos supposedly typed up by Bush's superior officer in the Guard, but a cursory glance from experts quickly revealed that the typeset of the alleged memos was in "Times New Roman." The significance?

This alleged memo was said to have been written on a typewriter, yet a closer look clearly indicated it was created on a modern computer using Microsoft Word's standard Times New Roman font. It was an obvious fraud, and for Dan Rather and the folks at 60 minutes, things only got worse from there!

Soon CBS was forced to retract the story and Dan Rather himself personally apologized for his role. This was a case of fake news that was at least owned up to at the time. Dan Rather seemed to regret his apology shortly thereafter however, when he became defensive about the debacle.

Painting himself as a victim, he criticized the bloggers who exposed the error of his ways, calling them "powerful and extremely well-financed forces who decided to attack him and destroy his credibility." Well, so much for taking responsibility for one's own actions and journalism integrity.

In his later defense of his journalistic discretions, Rather set a precedent for those who followed in his footsteps. Since then it has become standard procedure for media outlets caught reporting fake news to double down, deny blame, cast aspersions on their critics, and make excuses.

Now flash forward a little over ten years later to 2015, when then NBC Nightly News host, Brian Williams, came under fire for flagrantly supplying his own brand of "alternative facts" to his journalistic arsenal.

Williams, who was known to add plenty of flash to his speech, was suddenly caught in bold-faced lie. In a dramatic retelling of his visit to Iraq in 2003, he claimed that he touched down under heavy artillery fire. Those who were there with him quickly refuted this story by stating that there was no such barrage when Brian Williams had landed. Plus, others immediately contested it as well

As was the case with Dan Rather when the truth came out, Brian Williams apologized and his network took action. In this case removing Williams from his vaunted position as lead anchor of NBC Nightly News and relegating him to a more minor role as a breaking news anchor on MSNBC.

In these two primary examples, the news networks seemed (on the surface at least) to take violations of journalistic honesty and integrity pretty seriously. But one way or another, after the 2016 election these standards seemed to change. Why would I say that?

Well, the big fake elephant in the room is the Steel dossier. What is the Steel dossier? It's basically a set of memos that came about when a think tank group, Fusion GPS, working on behalf of Hillary Clinton and the DNC, hired a British former spy by the name of Michael Steele who was knowledgeable with Russian affairs, and used him in an attempt to dig up dirt on Donald Trump.

For those who were following the Impeachment hearings of 2019, it might strike them as rather ironic (and perhaps hypocritical) that while Donald Trump was being investigated for using a foreign agent (the president of Ukraine) to dig up dirt on a political rival, Hillary Clinton had done the same thing during the 2016 campaign.

Hillary of course was not an elected official at the time, and she was not withholding aid to Michael Steele in order to get what she wanted, but the similarities are striking just the same. At any rate, it was Michael Steele who compiled a whole dossier of allegations against Donald Trump, most of them so outlandish they are not even worth repeating.

As far-fetched and unfounded as the claims were however, they were apparently taken serious by the FBI. And the data was merited to be enough to help facilitate the launching of the initial Russia probe during the 2016 presidential campaign. After Trump was elected—the story was then leaked to the public through the blogging site newsfeed.com, just 10 days prior to the inauguration on January 10th, 2017.

Although many sharper minds knew that the veracity of the dossier was dubious at best, many mainstream news outlets took it at face value, including infamously enough, NBC Nightly News with Lester Holt. Mr. Holt reported this torrid innuendo with a straight face, as if the Steele dossier was a real and noteworthy news story.

But that wasn't the only fake or misleading news story of that year. For it was the same year that the NBC Nightly News tried to push the buttons of American viewers by airing a story about an American teenager who "stared" at a Native American activist. Yes, you read that correctly, primetime news was covering a story about an alleged staring contest.

But that's not the half of it. Or actually *NBC only played half of it*! Portraying teenage Donald Trump supporters visiting Washington DC as racist bullies who were harassing minorities; NBC played the tail end of a video that showed Native American activist Nathan Phillips playing a drum, and getting in teenager Nick Sandmann's face.

According to the news piece, we were supposed to believe that this young man had just mercilessly heckled the poor tribal elder. But it didn't take long for the truth to come out, and once the whole video and Sandmann's testimony emerged, an entirely different story came to light!

Sandmann and his friends were at a separate event in DC minding their own business when a radical group of black supremacists known as the "Black Israelites" (the same group that recently staged an attack on a Jewish store in Jersey City) had been mercilessly heckling Sandmann and his fellow students.

They apparently saw the Trump hats that the kids were wearing, and let it rip, calling them everything from "school shooters" to "future pedophiles". It was then that Native American activist Nathan Phillips stepped between the two groups as if he were perhaps trying to diffuse the situation. But in an odd showing, he decided to get right in Sandmann's face as he proceeded to chant and beat a drum.

It was an admittedly awkward situation, and Sandmann did what just about any teenager would; he smiled and laughed. But NBC News only played the last 15 seconds of the 2-minute video, without revealing the context of the situation. The story was then portrayed as if Sandmann was the aggressor, getting in Nathan Philips face, when in reality it was the other way around.

It's unclear how this misleading bit of fake news came about. Whether it was intentional or NBC was outright deceit by whoever submitted it? Yet in full damage control mode, Sandmann was invited on the Today Show a few days later to state his case. While on the show, the shocked and dismayed young man gave a heartfelt explanation that he never wanted to bother anyone; he was just there with his group and minding his own business when he was approached.

He also said that he would like to speak with Mr. Nathan Philips anytime, and he had nothing against him or anyone else (even though Philips in his haste to generate fake news, basically lied about the youngster on national TV). Few instances of media manipulation have distorted the truth recently as much as this piece did. And for what end exactly?

Ultimately, it was done to make Donald Trump look bad. There has been a concerted effort on the part of the media to promote any and every story that might present Trump in a bad light. So when such stories can't readily be found, it seems as though the fake news machinery of the media outright creates them.

In the same vein, perhaps even more infamously was the case of celebrity Jussie Smollet. Mr. Smollet, an actor from the popular TV series "Empire", made national news for several weeks on the claim that he was the victim of a hate crime committed by Trump supporters in Chicago.

This was just the kind of juicy anti-trump catnip the media was looking for! Once again, it's just too bad that the story they peddled wasn't actually true. As most of the world now knows, Smollet in fact staged his own hate crime! According to the Chicago police department, he hired a couple of his associates to jump him, rough him up, and put a noose around his neck.

The two men he hired (Abimbola and Olabinjo Osundairo) hailed from Nigeria and were body builders and sometimes extras on the set of Empire. Each of the men was allegedly paid $3500, for their role in staging the fake attack.

Found out for this frightening fraud, Smollet faced some pretty serious charges for creating his own fake news in an apparent attempt to smear Trump. But he lucked out in the end, since the crooked Cook

County State's Attorney, Kim Foxx, suddenly and surprisingly declared her refusal to press any charges against the disgraced actor.

In exchange for a mere 16 hours of community service and the "forfeiting of his $10,000 bond" that was paid to secure his release from jail, the case was thrown out. It was a whirlwind few weeks during the time that the media covered this fake news story. Since the story served to trash Trump and his supporters despite its false allegations, the networks couldn't wait to cover it.

So eager were they, that they didn't even do the most basic fact checking. They just took Smollet's word for it, when even the most casual observer could see flaws in Smollet's story from the very beginning. Smollet claimed that two white men wearing red Donald Trump hats jumped out of the shadows, punched him, and put a noose around his neck while shouting, "This is MAGA country!"

For many who heard this, the very idea of someone prowling around Chicago's inner-city with a MAGA hat on while claiming that it's "MAGA country" would seem patently absurd. Even Trevor Noah of the satirical news program, the Daily Show, admitted that such things were too funny for even HIM to make up.

Basically any rational person seemed to believe that there was something fishy about the Jussie Smollet story. Yet it took the fake news media several months to admit it. And in the words of the Chicago Police Chief, Eddie Johnson, who presided over the whole Jussie Smollet incident—"Bogus police reports cause real harm." Indeed they do, and so does fake news!

CHAPTER 7

Political Power to the People?

"The people have the power—all we have to do is awaken that power in the people. The people are unaware. They're not educated to realize that they have power. The system is so geared that everyone believes the government will fix everything. [But] we [the people]—are the government."

–JOHN LENNON

"POWER TO THE PEOPLE!" It's an encouraging expression that was first popularized in the mid-sixties and it also made for a pretty potent John Lennon song later on in the seventies. However, while it really is a nice idea does the American population really hold that kind of power? From to voters in the booths, to protesters in the streets, can the actions and intentions of average everyday people really sway the needle that much?

According to much of the doom and gloom on the left, it appears the answer is 'no'. Moreover, if you listened to the protesters with placards proclaiming, "We are the 99%!" and jockeying to disrupt the so-called elite 1%, you wouldn't think that we the people wielded very much power at all!

Amazingly in 2014, right when the 99%er movement began to really take off, Princeton University did a study to officially gauge how much say the average person had when it came to changing the status quo of government, and the results were alarming to say the least.

The folks at Princeton thoroughly went through approximately "two decades" of information on the state of the union and the power of the citizenry therein. What did they find? They discovered that while on the surface the average person appears to wield considerable political power via their vote and free speech, there are actually some rather dire impediments to these bastions of democracy.

According to these professors, "If policymaking is dominated by powerful business organizations and a small number of affluent Americans, then America's claims to being a Democratic society are seriously threatened."

They also asserted that "Not only do ordinary citizens not have uniquely substantial power over policy decisions; they have little or no independent influence on policy at all." Though the truth may hurt, there you have it!

Sure, the powers that be may throw the rest of us a bone every once and a while, but the meat is left to the top 1%, elite Americans. A prime example of this would be the primaries in a presidential election. I'm often amazed at how most people never seem to consider how voiceless most of the nation is when it comes the final determination of a political party's nominee.

Towards the end of a presidential election we routinely have two 'real' nominees, from two different political parties foisted upon us. We're basically left with two choices that the American people never really picked in the first place.

Since most of the electorate is not involved in the primary process, the majority of us are eventually presented with two candidates in the general election without any of our own input. Then we're basically told, "Alright! Pick the one you like best!"

In the 2016 election for example, a good number of Democrats were sincerely hoping Bernie Sanders would win the party's nomination, yet were somehow stuck with Hillary? How does this happen? It's basically because most of us do not participate in primaries. But just how is it that you participate in primary elections?

Primary voters are primarily (pardon the pun) older people and they are typically party affiliated. Some states don't require a primary voter to identify with a particular party beforehand, and those elections are termed "open", meaning that they are open contests in which anyone of any party can vote for any candidate.

This means that Republicans can try to pick the Democratic nominee, and known Democrats can try their luck picking who would be the Republican opponent. In fact, some have actually used this as an active strategy.

This is done by purposefully voting for the weakest candidate of the opposition party with the hopes that they'll become the nominee. Succeeding with this strategy would ideally open the door for their real preferred candidate of the party that they actually want to win, which could potentially lead to an easy victory in the general election (or at least that's what the ones employing the strategy must believe.)

Since the 2016 presidential election, some have even openly wondered if this strategy wasn't used in the matchup between Hillary Clinton and Donald Trump. Did some Democrats purposefully vote for Trump in the Republican primaries because they thought that Hillary would easily defeat him?

One thing that seems to support this theory is the fact that Trump always seemed to do better in open primaries. And as mentioned before, open primaries are contests in which voters do not have to be registered with the party of the candidates involved, so the voting is open to anyone regardless of party affiliation.

Were Democrats lining up in droves to vote for Trump in the open elections? Were they casting their ballots in a so-called effort of "strategic voting?" Some grumbling Republicans seemed to really believe this at the time, and as Trump continued to climb it became one of the variations attached to their cautionary cries of, "But—it's a trap!" when it came to voting for him.

Indeed, some people claimed the whole 2016 primary election was rigged on both sides in a massive effort to help Hillary. Some of those who sincerely voiced such outlandish claims even went so far as to say that Trump was a democratic plant from the very beginning. One that was put in place so that Hillary could easily defeat him.

As paranoid as such accusations might sound now, you can perhaps understand why someone would say that. Especially since Trump appears to be the complete antithesis of Hillary Clinton in many ways. Either way, it's no wonder that some would of thought she could easily beat him.

In fact, Trump clashes with Hillary so severely on several issues that you would think it would cause more of her voters to rally around her cause, if only out of sheer aversion to Trump. But as much as one might think this, there were probably more people that genuinely appreciated Trump's talking points more than they did Hillary's.

At any rate, some form of this so-called strategic voting occurs in just about every election that entails open primaries. In order to avoid this very thing from happening, several states hold what are termed "closed" primaries. With this process the voters strictly have to proclaim what party they are affiliated with and can vote only for the candidate of that party. That way there is no strategic cross over.

Contrary to popular belief, the primary is not something that was established in the constitution. The current primary process was actually first developed around 1910. Many actually felt that the primary would be a great step up from the back room deals that party bosses had made in the past when it came to securing a nominee. But interestingly enough, there was one famous dissenter.

Henry Jones Ford, a political science professor from Princeton University had voiced his misgivings about the newly proposed process in a 1909 edition of "The North American Review." Here, he quite presciently made the statement, "The idea which commends the direct primary to the masses is that it is a means of giving power to the people."

The esteemed professor then went on to assert, that although these were the intentions of a primary, the results could turn out to be quite the opposite. And instead of giving power to the people, they could very well, "take advantage and opportunity from one set of politicians and confer them upon another set."

In another words, a primary would be rather selective in just what set of people wield that said political power. And this is precisely what we have seen played out in the past few presidential elections. In both parties the primary voter tends to be college educated, trending toward those that have finished graduate school and often have high incomes.

There is of course nothing necessarily wrong with that, though the fact that it's the uber-educated and rich primarily voting in the primaries, essentially creates an elite class of king makers when it comes to determining a party's nominee. If the poorest people only vote in the general election, then they are always beholden to whoever and whatever the wealthy and well-connected of either party offer up to them.

Is this really 'power to the people' or is it really a select few wealthy elites that are calling all the shots? In the 2016 Democratic primary for example, many Bernie Sanders supporters felt disenfranchised to discover that the primary seemed to have already been bankrolled and secured for Hillary Clinton well in advance.

How do we know this? Mainly because of the hacked and leaked DNC emails! Released rightly or wrongly, these private messages between DNC leaders such as Donna Brazille and Debbie Wasserman Schultz were leaked to the public and it revealed outright bias for Clinton over Sanders in the primary.

Though this revelation created absolute chaos in the DNC Convention, Hillary was still nominated. And Bernie supporters who already suspected that the DNC was stacking the deck against him in favor of Hilary's imminent "coronation" by the party chair, now seemingly had their proof just as the primaries were coming to a close.

This led to enraged supporters standing at the convention grounds with sarcastic signs that read, "Thanks for your help Debbie"—which was of course in reference to the perceived help that Debbie and her elitist cronies provided to Hillary in the primaries while hurting Bernie's chances.

Presently, the debate over the effectiveness of primaries persists. And as of this writing, as the Democratic primary of 2020 comes to a close, many are probably holding their breath and wondering if the primary voter really knows what's best after all?

But of course, as important as the vote is—voting is not the only political power that the American people hold in their hands. The tenants of free speech in this country allow for protests and certain demonstrations of civil disobedience. And as any good activist knows, if certain issues are not dealt with at the ballot box then they just might have to be taken to the streets!

The Reverend Martin Luther King Jr. was one of the most renowned Civil Rights activists of all time. And as much as Dr. King encouraged citizens to vote, he also encouraged them to peacefully march on important issues. In a search for justice and equality, he and his followers marched on many places. Perhaps most famous was the Job and Freedom March on Washington, D.C. in 1963.

These efforts helped to pave the way for landmark Civil Rights legislation being carried out in the 1960's. By the end of his career, King had already achieved a whole lot. But right before he was tragically shot and killed by an assassin in 1968, Martin Luther King had one of his greatest power to the people campaigns in the works. He called it the "Poor People's Campaign."

In this movement he envisioned a diverse coalition derived from the lower classes that included impoverished whites in Appalachia, inner-city African Americans, struggling rural farmers, and the like, all joining together and taking to the streets in order to demand the opportunity for a better livelihood in the American economy.

Perhaps the idea of a bunch of poor people rising up with real political power in their hands, didn't sit too well with the elite establishment, but Dr. King was ready and willing to proceed regardless. Sadly, he was prevented from fulfilling this final mission of his.

However, recently a revived poor people's campaign was established by Civil Rights activist Reverend William Barber. Reverend Barber is a true believer in the power of the people and has went on the record to state, "People should not live in or die from poverty in the richest nation ever to exist."

Currently, the new campaign is busy organizing cross-country tours. These tours are intended to spread awareness of the financial plight of lower income families and the latent political power that those same poor people could potentially possess someday.

As the movement picks up steam, several 2020 Democratic presidential candidates have been invited along for the ride, including Elizabeth Warren, Bernie Sanders, and Pete Buttigieg—just to name a few.

With such wide coverage of this movement, it just goes to show you that average everyday people, including the poorest among us, do indeed hold considerable political power; they merely have to properly make use of it!

CHAPTER 8

Just How Accurate is Polling Data?

"If the critics are right that I've made all my decisions based on polls, then I must not be very good at reading them."
–President Barack Obama

IN TODAY'S SOCIETY WE hear poll results rattled off on a recurring basis, and they're often regarding politics. For instance, we're told this politician is polling better than that one, or this particular special interest is viewed more favorably in recent polling data.

Pollsters make a living gathering knee-jerk reactions, then tallying and grouping them into a conglomerate of information that is supposed to quantify a majority sentiment. But just how accurate are these polls? Well, as much as some politicians would like to use polls to predict their future, they can be shockingly far from accurate!

This was actually spectacularly proven in the 2016 election when Donald Trump defied all the odds (and the tabulated polling data) by securing an unexpected and dramatic electoral victory over Hillary Clinton. This proves the polling data that was relied upon to 'check the pulse' of the average American voter was clearly incorrect.

So, it certainly does beg the big question—just how accurate is any polling data in the first place? One of the major flaws of polls is that in part they depend on something that no pollster can properly discern.

And that is—just how honest and/or easily swayed are the people that they're polling?

It was the 2016 presidential election after all that revealed the now infamous "hidden Trump voter." These voters were allegedly the type that would feel social pressure to deny their support for Trump when prompted in person, or even over the phone by a pollster. Yet in the privacy of a voting booth, they confidently cast their vote for him.

In many ways, the phenomenon of the hidden trump voter shouldn't be all that surprising. Trump, whether rightly or wrongly, was made out to be such a deplorable villain that to some, admitting admiration for him seemed akin to admitting admiration for Genghis Khan.

In other words, in order to avoid looks of disdain and imminent social ostracism, the hidden Trump voters publicly denied their support of Trump. Yet deep down they agreed with many of his ideas, no matter how much the news media and the left attempted in pressuring them not to.

Another factor that can skew voting results is simply when pollsters do not include enough people from the opposition party. Polls conducted in 2019 have demonstrated this flaw when pairing democratic candidates against President Trump's chances for re-election.

For example, one poll conducted in the summer of 2019 asked voters how they would vote when pairing Trump with Biden, Warren, and Sanders. At first the poll seemed to have Trump trailing all of the candidates, but the results were completely misleading.

Because if someone were to dig a little bit deeper into how the poll was conducted, they would find that of those polled, 43% were avowed Democrats while 33% were avowed Republicans. With this taken into consideration, if all the voters remained true to their party base, out of this lopsided example, one could only expect a lopsided result.

It didn't necessarily mean that Trump was trailing behind on a national level, just within one small focus group in which the odds were stacked against him. But one of the most glaring test cases for unreliable polling data was undoubtedly the 2016 presidential election.

Because in 2016, almost all of the final polls before the votes were cast had indicated Hillary as the most likely winner. In the aftermath of this colossal misconception, three main factors have been blamed for the discrepancy.

First of all, as mentioned earlier, due to the social pressure they felt, not all Trump voters were ready to openly admit they were going to vote for him. This resulted in crucial percentage points for Trump going largely unaccounted for. Secondary to this was the fact that support for Trump seemed to spike in the very last days of the campaign.

In addition to these two known issues; university grads seemed to have been over-sampled for many of the polls. And as it so happened, college grads in many cases tended to trend toward Clinton more than Trump. Because of this, their overrepresentation in the polls created an artificial boost for Hillary.

Also, a big part of the overall problem in the 2016 polls is that the pollsters relied more on national feedback rather than state-based feedback. National poll casting is insightful for the popular vote but that's not taking the Electoral College into consideration. This was clearly evidenced in 2016.

Because polls that had Hillary ahead by a couple of percentage points were actually pretty close to the end result when it came to the *popular vote,* which in itself is a national referendum. But when it came to Electoral College states to be won, the polls incorrectly predicted wins for Hillary in a few Trump states such as Michigan and Ohio, and this is where the real problem with the polls occurred.

And if it was inaccurate then, could it be any better now? As of the writing of this book, on the eve of the 2020 elections, significant efforts are said to be underway to ensure more accurate polling results. Of course there are skeptics, and one of them is Courtney Kennedy, an analyst from the Pew Research Center.

As recently as 2019, Ms. Kennedy went on the record to state that she didn't "see an infusion of high-quality state level polls that weren't there in 2016." In other words, national polls remain the better funded of the two, and without additional funding and support, state polling is still bound to produce inaccurate results.

On the bright side, if the 2018 midterm elections were any kind of a proving ground for polling, it is said that the results conducted by pollsters in the midterm matchups were found to be by and large correct.

Most of the candidates projected for a big win on election night, did indeed go on to an electoral victory. We can only hope in 2020 and beyond that this trend of fair and balanced (and more importantly, *accurate*) efforts in polling will continue.

The more cynical however, might wonder if trolling data might actually supersede efficient polling *data*. Traditional political polling is done through phone calls, or other surveys which adhere to a certain set of parameters such as an agreed upon sample size of those polled, the selection process involved, and the inherent margin of data.

But trolling data, that my dear readers is a whole different animal entirely. The political trolls gather on social media and flood the system with either repeated manual entries or with the help of programmed bots built to wreak all kinds of havoc. So what happens when similar measures are implemented to attack online polling?

This phenomenon came to the forefront in the summer of 2019 during the first series of Democratic presidential debates for the 2020 primaries. It was discovered that shortly after one of the debates, trolls flooded message boards in an effort to get users to cast votes for Marianne Williamson and Andrew Yang, who were actually the two most marginal candidates at the time.

They did this through blatant advertising and recruiting. One message board declared to all who came across it, "Vote for Yang in this poll. He needs to win in every poll we can find." This became what amounted to a troll backed coordination campaign for a candidate.

Obviously, Andrew Yang didn't have any control or even know about these efforts being carried out on his behalf, but the results were rather startling all the same.

In a poll conducted by the Drudge Report, Yang actually came in 1st place. This is a feat that would eventually astonish even Andrew Yang himself. After all, he was a new face and had spoken on stage for less than three minutes at the previous debate. Yet, he suddenly skyrocketed to the top position in the polls?

Yang was also a definite underdog going into the debate, achieving only about 1 percent in previous polling. So how in the world could he go from 1 percent to 100 percent?

Even worse, some well-known news publications such as the "Daily Caller" failed to fact-check the veracity of this erroneous polling data while publishing gushing accounts of Yang's monumental rise in the polls as if it were scientific fact, when it was more like science fiction!

Online polls are unfortunately unreliable tools, especially since so many nameless responders can 'game the system'. This is why most respected pollsters refrain from open online polling. They only use a designated sample of the populace that is chosen beforehand from which they extract their data and share it. So, exactly how accurate is polling data? As you can see, a large part of it simply depends on exactly who is doing the polling.

CHAPTER 9

Justice OR Witch Hunt?

"You should read history and look at ostracism, persecution, martyrdom, and that kind of thing. They always happen to the best men, you know."
–George Eliot

THE AMERICAN PLEDGE OF Allegiance ends with the words, "…one nation under God, indivisible, with liberty and justice for all." It certainly was the intention of the founding fathers for the United States to have a fair and equitable system of justice in which truth would be the priority and facts would prevail over opinion and hearsay, or simply suspicion.

However, in today's polarized political landscape that's loaded with whistleblowers, political theatre, and highly partisan kangaroo courts that sometimes seem more similar to the tribunals and show trials of the Soviet Union than any fair and meaningful judicial process, one cannot help but wonder if we've somehow missed the mark?

On December 18th, 2019, Donald J. Trump, the 45th President of the United States was impeached by the House of Representatives. With Democrats in control of the house, the vote was by and large along party lines with only two of them voting not to impeach and another Democratic congresswoman, Tulsi Gabbard, staying out of the fray altogether by simply marking "present".

So it was, with virtually all of the Republican Party against it (and a few Democratic dissenters) that the house Democrats impeached the president, making Trump one of only three U.S. presidents in history to have been impeached. This of course is not the end of the story however, as after impeachment there is still a trial that must be held in the Senate, which will determine whether or not the president will be removed from office.

Although the impeachment hearings in the house moved at a rapid pace, it seems Democratic House leader Nancy Pelosi has since decided that delaying the proceedings might prove to be useful when it comes to the Senate trial. Pelosi has reasoned that she wants to hold-off until she can be reassured that the Senate Republicans will hold a fair trial for impeachment.

Yet some of the more cynical have suggested that maybe she's simply holding off until she can ensure that the Democrats have a majority in the Senate, with which they'll have the power to convict the president! Pelosi for her part claims that the holdup is primarily due to the fact that the White House has refused to allow key members of Trump's inner-circle to testify. Among these individuals are Secretary of State Mike Pompeo, acting Chief of Staff Mick Mulvaney, and former National Security adviser, John Bolton.

In her view, without these key members testifying, the trial would not be fair. Well that begs the question—was it ever fair to begin with? In order to answer that, let's go over what actually transpired. All of this latest impeachment hullabaloo began over a phone call President Trump made to the newly elected president of Ukraine on July 25th, 2019.

The call starts out with Trump congratulating Ukrainian President Zelensky on his recent election win. Zelensky who was previously a comedian and Ukrainian celebrity ran a populist style campaign somewhat similar to Trump's, which is something that they both acknowledge in the phone call.

After this initial chit-chat subsides, the two then get into discussing the political situation between Ukraine, Russia, the EU, and the United

States. Ukraine, which used to be joined at the hip with Russia in the Soviet Union, has been an independent country since the breakup of the Soviet Empire in 1991.

In recent times however, the Russian Federation has been trying to put pressure on Ukraine to return to the fold. And ever since the fall of the Russian backed Ukrainian President Viktor Yanukovych in 2014, Russia has been flexing their muscles in the region. In fact, it was shortly thereafter when Russia sent in troops to secure the important strategic base of the Crimean Peninsula.

This was supposedly to protect pro-Russian citizens as much as it was to secure this mighty military asset. At least, according to the talking points of Vladimir Putin, the denizens of Crimea wanted to rejoin Mother Russia. To prove this sentiment, Crimea actually held a vote in which the citizens of the Crimea Peninsula allegedly voted to join Russia, although the results have been viewed with great skepticism.

It was after this that Russia annexed Crimea—a piece of real estate that has shifted hands between Russia and Ukraine for centuries. This wasn't the end however, as Russian backed rebels continued to wage a war against the Ukrainian military, threatening to takeover and annex even more territory for Russia.

It is this ongoing threat that the newly elected Ukrainian President Zelensky faces, and in the July 25th, 2019 phone call, he turned to the topic and praised the U.S. for its support. Both he and Trump agreed that the United States was doing more for Ukraine than the EU, even though ostensibly, due to logistics the European Union should be doing a whole lot more.

Zelensky once again thanked Trump for all his help and then went on to state that he was especially interested in buying some Javelin missiles (a kind of tank busting weapon) from the United States to use in its ongoing efforts against Russia. It was at this point that Trump infamously stated, "I would like you to do us a favor though, because our country has been through a lot and Ukraine knows a lot about it."

Trump then went on to state, "I would like you to find out

what happened with this whole situation with Ukraine, they say CrowdStrike.... You have one of your wealthy people... The server, they say Ukraine has it. There are a lot of things that went on, the whole situation. I think you're surrounding yourself with some of the same people. I would like to have the Attorney General call you or your people. I would like you to get to the bottom of it."

This request by President Trump for Zelensky to "do him a favor" could seemingly be viewed in at least two ways, depending on your perspective. Trump supporters and many other Republicans see nothing wrong with what they believe to be nothing more than one president asking another to investigate potential corruption in his own country. But Democrat observers see this as the leadup to a shakedown, especially since in the very next sentence, Trump brings up the findings of the Mueller Report.

Trump continued, "As you saw yesterday, that whole nonsense ended with a very poor performance by a man named Robert Mueller, an incompetent performance, but they say a lot of it started with Ukraine. Whatever you can do, it's very important that you do it if that's possible."

After reading the transcript of this phone call, you just might think that President Trump is one of the most unquotable people on the face of the Earth. This is because he speaks in very vague and circular language. In just a short time he rambles through a lot of different subjects.

,So, in the phone call Zelensky praised Trump for the aid he'd had already given him and mentioned that he would like additional military aid in the form of Javelin missiles. Trump then basically responds by telling him that's all well and good, but he would like for Zelensky/Ukraine to do him a favor.

He never demanded a favor, he just opened his remarks with that suggestion and then launched into a longwinded talk on several different topics. He mentions that "our country had been through a lot." And then makes statements about "CrowdStrike."

First of all, what the heck is CrowdStrike? Well, it is the name of a cybersecurity service that the DNC used during the 2016 presidential election. It was these supposed cybersecurity experts that the Democrats had first tasked with looking into the hacking of their emails. It has been suspected however, that CrowdStrike, instead of aiding in this task may have conducted an "inside job" and actually began hacking the DNC, as well as "planting" evidence to make it look like it was the Russians who did it.

CrowdStrike also has connections with Ukraine in its efforts to safeguard Ukrainian assets from the Russians. This is the link that supposedly brings Ukraine into the picture when it comes to hacking and interference with the 2016 elections. To be clear, many believe all of this to be a complete conspiracy theory.

But even if this theory sounds completely misplaced and far-fetched, in the aftermath of Trump's phone call, the reaction of the media has been somewhat surprising. Many have questioned why the media is so quick to shoot the theory down? Not only without question, but without even explaining what CrowdStrike is and what the theory behind it is all about (conspiracy or not).

Any mention about this portion of the call and news anchor's suddenly dismiss it and declare some variation of, "CrowdStrike—it's a crazy conspiracy theory—we're not even going to get into that." If it really were so crazy, you would think that the media could at least explain why. That way viewers would better understand what's going on and come to their own conclusion.

It's their job after all to inform the public, but most news outlets seem like they wish to speak as little about it as possible. And the same goes for any mention of Joe Biden, who happens to be the second main subject of this now infamous phone call. Again, the media for the most part refuses to go into any detail as to why Trump mentioned Biden's name.

When it comes to Biden, all the talking heads do is solemnly proclaim, "Joe Biden—he's been cleared of any wrong doing. That theory's been debunked." The media seems content to tell the public what to believe without giving any rationale or reason why. Their reactions are somewhat akin to a defense attorney at a trial for an accused killer, proclaiming, "My client's innocent. That's all you need to know. Now shut-up and don't worry about it!"

If someone has such a deep-set belief in something, you would expect they'd at least give a somewhat convincing explanation. Or perhaps the media's routine reaction is more like a parent whom after their child asks, "But why?" responds, "Because I said so!"

The topics of CrowdStrike and Biden (for whatever reason) are viewed as so sacred, that they can't even be mentioned for more than 2 seconds of airtime by the press. And pretty much anyone who looks into it any further is basically considered a nutty conspiracy theorist. Our custodians in the media have seemingly deemed us all unworthy of knowing anything further about the actual facts.

At any rate, as the phone call continued, the next main topic was indeed Joe Biden. Trump and Zelensky had mentioned efforts to combat corruption in Ukraine and then spoke at some length about a certain Ukrainian prosecutor "who was very good" at fighting corruption but was "shut down" and how that was "really unfair."

The prosecutor they spoke of in this exchange was Viktor Shokin, who was fired upon the recommendation of then Vice President Joe Biden, though the 'official story' may differ. Opening up that particular can of worms, Trump goes on to state, "There's a lot of talk about Biden's son, that Biden stopped the prosecution and a lot of people want to find out about that, so whatever you can do with the Attorney General would be great. Biden went around bragging that he stopped the prosecution so if you can look into it.... It sounds horrible to me."

This is supposedly where Trump pressured the Ukrainian president to investigate Joe Biden and his son Hunter Biden's connections with Ukraine. The connection being that of Hunter's work on the board of a Ukrainian gas company called Burisma while his father was vice president. Burisma was being investigated for corruption until Joe Biden "shut it down" by having the acting prosecutor fired.

How did Joe Biden have the prosecutor fired? By withholding aid to Ukraine of course. Because you see while Trump has been routinely lambasted as a criminal for allegedly withholding aid underhandedly, Biden openly did so! Not only that, but his actions have been hailed as "highly appropriate methods to pressure Ukraine."

It was supposedly in an effort to "do the right thing" when Biden requested Ukraine's top prosecutor, Shokin be fired. Biden withheld over 1 billion dollars in loan guarantees for Ukraine until his condition was met. In fact, it was these efforts that Biden actually "bragged" about in front of a live audience.

In a recent speech, Biden told an audience of how he had declared to Ukrainian officials, "I'm leaving in six hours. If the prosecutor is not fired, you're not getting the money. Well, son of a bitch. He got fired." This is what Biden openly admitted to in his role of having former Ukrainian prosecutor, Viktor Shokin fired.

As suspicious as these actions seem to just about anyone who hears them, this is the very situation that the press keeps loudly proclaiming to be completely clear of "any wrong doing." However, when Trump asks Zelensky to do him a favor by looking into these matters, far from seeming pressured or reluctant, Zelensky adamantly agrees that the matter needs attending.

Zelensky goes on to state, "I wanted to tell you about the prosecutor. First of all, I understand and I'm knowledgeable about the situation. Since we have won the absolute majority in our Parliament, the next prosecutor general will be 100% my person, my candidate, who will be approved by parliament and will start as a new prosecutor in September. He or she will look into the situation, specifically to the company that you mentioned in this issue. The issue of the investigation of the case is actually the issue of making sure to restore the honesty, so we will take care of that and will work on the investigation of the case."

Despite what anyone might want to infer, there really is no

solid quid quo pro in the sense that Trump didn't directly order the Ukrainian president to do anything. He simply made the suggestion that he'd appreciate it if they could look into a few things. And there was zero resistance from Zelensky whatsoever, the Ukrainian President immediately agreed that it would be a good idea to follow up on the issues Trump suggested.

Zelensky after all, had run on a platform in which he pledged to clear up corruption in Ukraine. Looking into the alleged corruption of Burisma would simply be part and parcel to what he had already promised to do upon being elected president.

The thing that Democrats pounced on was the fact that Trump withheld the military aid including the Javelin missiles shortly after this phone call. They have made the claim that Trump was trying to turn the military aid into some kind of incentive or in their words "bribe" in order to ensure Zelensky carried out the investigations he had already promised to do on the July 25th phone call.

But as Republicans have already pointed out during the impeachment hearings, Zelensky at no point even realized that the aid was being withheld. And so that obviously begs the question, if Zelensky didn't even know the aid was being withheld, then how in the world was Trump pressuring Zelensky?

From Zelensky's perspective nothing had changed and everything was going forward as usual with Ukraine set to receive the promised military aid in September of 2019. It wasn't until the so-called whistleblower came out and this whole debacle was front page news, that Zelensky knew anything about it.

Some Democratic lawmakers at the impeachment hearings scoffed at the notion of "no harm, no foul", considering Trump to be guilty of "attempted extortion." They have claimed that Trump was trying to extort the Ukraine and only ceased and desisted with his efforts when exposed by the whistleblower.

While it is true that the release of the aid occurred shorty after the whistleblower came out, this does not prove extortion was the motive for withholding it. After all, in order to extort someone, the other party must be aware that they are being extorted. And as already mentioned, Zelensky, the President of Ukraine had no idea the aid was being delayed.

Democrats tried to liken the president's actions to a bank robber attempting to rob a bank, but seeing the police pull up, threw down his gun and ran out empty handed. Or as one Democratic representative put it, "Attempted robbery is just as much a crime as actual robbery."

What the Democrats are really trying to do here is basically charge the president with a "thought crime." In other words, these thought police are apparently able to read the president's mind and somehow know exactly what he was thinking when he paused the delivery of the aid package to Ukraine.

Trump never directly said he was pausing the aid because he was trying to force an investigation into CrowdStrike and the Bidens, this is merely the Democrats interpretation. Even if the timing of it looks terrible, there is no way anyone can definitely determine Trump's motives or prove exactly what was going through his mind when he halted the aid.

Having said that, rather than an aborted bank robbery, a better analogy could go a little something like this. Let's say that a mugger was standing on a city corner staring at someone he wanted to mug. At this point the person he was considering mugging wasn't even aware they were an intended target. But then Nancy Pelosi walked right up and making use of her incredible psychic gifts, read the assailants mind, figured out his intentions before he acted on them, and promptly called in the cops to have him arrested for allegedly thinking about an act he didn't actually commit.

Sound ridiculous? Well, that's basically the whole basis of the Democratic hearing that has led to Trump's impeachment in the House of Representatives. All throughout the hearing everything they had against Trump was based on secondhand accounts, inferences, and assumptions of what others felt Trump meant when he used vague words such as "favor."

The truth is, there isn't any solid evidence indicating that Trump did anything wrong. Admittedly, even if Trump did indeed have nefarious intentions, Trump is notoriously catty and vague in his language, making it extraordinarily hard to entrap him in anything. Sometimes the president sounds like he talks in riddles while going from one thing to another, in a completely jumbled up word salad.

This is precisely what drives his Democratic opponents absolutely insane. Because as much as they want to infer and speculate as to what the president's intentions are, they always seem to fall short and just end up making themselves look like silly, hyperventilating basket cases in the process. Nevertheless, on the flimsy basis of what the Democratic controlled House "interpreted" Trump's phone call to mean—the 45th President, Donald J. Trump was impeached!

Currently the Republicans still hold control of the Senate, which makes it highly unlikely that Trump will be convicted and removed from office. But Nancy Pelosi seems like she has some final tricks up her sleeve. She's delaying the senate trial until she deems that the process is going to be fair in the Senate. Could she really be waiting to see if the 2020 election results will bring back a Democratic majority in the Senate?

Then again, if she pushes her luck she might just hang onto those articles of impeachment until she herself gets voted out of office. Either way, according to one of the Constitutional Law professors that testified during the hearing, Trump has technically not been impeached until Pelosi sends the articles over to the Senate and a trial convenes.

As much as Democratic house members were cheering and high fiving each other on December 19th, 2019, if she refuses to take this step, it will basically be as if Trump was never impeached in the first place. The search to impeach Trump—is it justice? Or is it a wild and hysterical partisan witch hunt run amuck? It's possible we may never know the answer to that, regardless of the impeachment outcome.

CHAPTER 10

The Real Reason Trump Got Elected

"An election is a moral horror, as bad as a battle except for the blood, a mud bath for every soul concerned in it."
—George Bernard Shaw

EVER SINCE THE RESULTS of the 2016 election rocked the nation, shocked liberals on the left have been scratching their heads trying to figure out just how it was that Trump got elected. Some have cited the economy and the fact that Trump's business acumen may have appealed to many. Others thought that maybe Trump was a wild card and outsider who they hoped would shakeup the establishment.

There were also those who tended to view the President in the worst possible light, taking on a pessimistic view that it was simply the more debased nature of the electorate (again, the Hillary designated deplorables) coming out of the woodwork to elect the brash billionaire.

Still others however, refused to accept or admit that Trump was fairly elected at all, and began to truly believe that his surprise victory was the result of Russian interference into the election. Furthermore, some were (and still are) certain that the Trump campaign actively colluded with the Russians in order to win the election.

Former FBI Director Robert Mueller's infamous report dropped in the spring of 2019 found no evidence of collusion. In fact, the only Russian interference they discovered was an intense social media campaign seeking to affect the opinions of American voters through platforms such as Facebook.

But even though Russian bots may have been routinely trolling social media sites, no Russian intelligence had any access whatsoever to American voter booths. The voting machines were not hacked or in any way compromised, and every single vote cast was done so by the freewill of the American voter. So, if it wasn't the Russians that got Trump elected—then who was it?

Many believe it was the disaffected working class of Middle America who felt regularly discarded by elitist politicians and disregarded by the mainstream media. This was the main group that Trump motivated to take action with his populist message.

Trump ran on a platform in which he promised to bring jobs back. He touted his past experience as both a real estate mogul and as a celebrity personality while presenting himself as the ultimate job creator. He once even made the grandiose exclamation "I will be the greatest job president God ever created." To the disbelief of liberals, this ridiculous sounding statement was met with cheers, prompting the Liberal Left to openly wonder—Is the Trump base just too stupid to see through his hubris?

But what these Democrats don't realize is that the working-class voters they often belittle consider the reactions of the Left in the same way, "Are liberals too serious to have a sense of humor?"

Because real Trump fans vibe with the president's sense of humor and they know that he is joking (we hope) when he makes such ridiculous statements. At the same time however, the Trump crowd truly does have faith that he will deliver on his promise when it comes to jobs as well as other issues.

And when it comes to bringing jobs back, it really doesn't seem to be a joke after all, because under Trump's administration unemployment has dropped to 3.6%. This marks a "50-year low" not seen since 1969. That's pretty impressive, especially considering that the previous Obama administration had an unemployment rate as high as 10% during his first term in office.

During the Obama years, even when the unemployment numbers finally did go down, they largely did so because Obama infused the economy with a deluge of part-time jobs. Many people then found themselves having to work two, or in some cases even three part-time jobs, just to survive or make a decent living.

Trump's seeming ability to bring back jobs, is indeed a high incentive for the working-class base to support him. While the Democrat's priority seemed to have shifted away from jobs and the economy, Trump and his cohorts have remained laser focused on these issues.

The argument can be made that matters of the economy used to be the Democrat's bread & butter when it came to the issues they chose to campaign on. In fact, it was Bill Clinton who made famous the campaign quip, "It's the economy, stupid." back in 1992.

This was the Clinton's blunt way of reminding everyone that his number one priority in running for president was supposedly to repair the economy and bring back jobs. But over recent years, the Democratic platform changed and shifted away from jobs. Instead of focusing on gaining favor with the working class by focusing on the economy, Democrats began playing games with identity politics, culture wars, immigration, the 1st & 2nd Amendments, and more...

Meanwhile, an elite cadre of wealthy Democratic progressives on both coasts and in Silicon Valley are working overtime to fulfill an agenda of their own. And what is that agenda? Centralized control certainly seems to be a big factor. Centralized control and dare I say it, yes certain aspects of socialism seem to be the goals of some in the current incarnation of the Democratic Party.

Some may not go so far as to say that the Democrats have become outright socialists, but it certainly seems to be trending in that direction. Bernie Sanders put a spotlight on this inclination in 2016 by openly running as a "Democratic Socialist." Such a thing would have been unheard of in prior presidential elections.

Ever since old Bernie set the stage, Democratic Socialists seem to be coming out of the woodwork in Washington, D.C. and elsewhere The new yet already well-known congresswoman recently elected in New York by the name of Alexandria Ocasio-Cortez (aka AOC) is a full-fledged supporter of socialist policy.

Ms. Cortez has advocated for the government to step in and control many aspects of the economy and society that previously would have been unheard of. Her decidedly ambitious Green New Deal for example, calls upon the U.S. to give up fossil fuel within 10 years and become completely beholden to renewable sources of energy.

Clean energy? That's great! Even most Republicans would probably agree that cleaner is better, but the means in which AOC intends to accomplish this task are implausible and downright frightening. The cost of this major governmental intervention would be around 2.5 billion dollars annually!

How does this budding socialist plan to pay for it? Why by taking a tip from the playbook of Vladimir Lenin himself—forcibly taking it from the rich! Her plan entails a wealth tax that would make the folks at higher income levels in this country have to carry the costliest burden of transitioning into the 100% Green Economy that AOC envisions.

Interestingly enough, this is a socialist tenant that others including Elizabeth Warren actually agree with. Warren has gone on the record to state that she would love to create a brand-new tax aimed specifically at targeting the wealthiest of Americans. And she does indeed refer to it as being a "wealth tax." Democrats believe that taking from the rich and giving to the poor is going to endear them with the lower classes, but most working-class attentive Americans see through this charade.

Most people don't want a handout from the government, at least not when it's derived by leeching money from the rich. Most just want a good job—one that is stable, and productive and allows them to give back to society on their own accord. Trump understands this sentiment, which is likely a major reason why he was elected in the first place.

Along with jobs however, for many the candidacy of Trump represented much more than that. He was viewed as an outsider that would shakeup the political establishment. Trump began his campaign in a very unorthodox manner, and the more he went against the grain, it seemed the more his supporters were endeared to him.

Trump not only took on the Democratic establishment, but also the establishment of his own party. In 2016, Republican Never Trumpers were a real thing, and Trump was nearly rejected by the Republicans and almost passed over for nomination.

It was only when the Republican establishment realized that they wouldn't be able to handle the fallout from angry voters and their own constituents if they dumped Trump, that they decided to finally give in and allow their most popular candidate to rightfully take the nomination for the party.

As much as Trump was beloved by his base however, one would be remiss to not mention that part of Trump's success was in fact due to the lackluster performance and reception of Hillary Clinton. Quite honestly, Hillary was just not as popular of a candidate in 2016 as Obama was in 2012, or even as she herself was back in 2008.

Sure, you could blame it on a number of things including leaked emails, her poor choice of words, or sheer Clinton burnout, but in 2016 she simply wasn't generating enough interest among Democratic voters. Some perhaps were those who were upset over the treatment of Bernie Sanders, and by the time of the general election, many even made a conscious decision to sit out the election entirely and not vote at all.

In this way, many who would have otherwise voted democratic, essentially voted neutral, and in doing so may have unwittingly given Trump a little bit of an edge over Hillary. By November of 2016, there were many frustrated voters who while in no way, shape or form would have voted for Trump, found that they were unable to bring themselves to vote for Hillary Clinton either.

Perhaps some even secretly liked Trump, and while they couldn't go so far as to cast their vote for him, many made sure they didn't vote for Clinton either. Whatever the case may be, Hillary received a much lower volume of the voting electorate in 2016 than Obama did in 2012

Though perhaps the most important reason Trump was elected could boil down to plain and simple frustration of the electorate. It has been proven time and time again that after 8 years of one party being in power, it is more difficult for a successor candidate of that said party to actually win the next election.

The last time that this feat was achieved was during the presidential election of 1988. Republican President Ronald Reagan had just finished up 8 years in the White House and his former VP and chosen successor George H. W. Bush managed to squeak out a win against the Democratic candidate Michael Dukakis.

But the odds for such a thing occurring for the Democratic Party seem even slimmer, as the last time a successor candidate succeeded was shortly before the Civil War way back in 1856! It's just the baked in habit of the American electorate to get tired of the same old party after 8 years, and after President Barack Obama finished up his 2nd term, many people were simply looking for that ever-elusive "change."

Perhaps this was part of the DNC's reasoning in selecting Hillary Clinton as their nominee instead of recruiting Obama's vice president, Joe Biden. Maybe it was believed that Clinton would provide more of a new direction than Biden, who had already spent the previous 8 years in the White House with Obama.

It could be that the DNC took a bit of a gamble with Hillary, hoping that she could generate enough interest to get Democrats to come out in sufficient enough numbers to keep the Democratic Party in power. Perhaps they felt that since Hillary was the first woman to win the nomination of a major political party, she would especially gain support from one of the Democrats key constituents—women!

But the candidacy of Hillary Clinton proved to not generate much excitement from either men or women of the Democrat Party. Hillary herself believes that the reason she lost the election was mainly due to rampant corruption and malfeasance on the part of the DNC!

Although the DNC was clearly supporting Hillary, according to Mrs. Clinton, that support didn't amount to much. In her book, "What Happened?" Hillary examined line-by-line, every single item she believed that affected her prospects of winning the election. One of the biggest reasons on the list was her claim that the DNC was left absolutely desolate by her Democratic predecessors.

She stated that shortly after she became the nominee, she told herself, "[Here I am] now the nominee of the Democratic Party. I inherit nothing from the Democratic Party. It was bankrupt… I had to inject money into the DNC to keep it going."

She paints a picture of a DNC in ruins; the results of slash and burn tactics from the previous leadership of the party. Is any of this true? It is a fact that the DNC was struggling at the beginning of the 2016 presidential campaign. And Hillary is indeed being honest when she states that it was her financial contributions that helped to keep it all afloat.

Of course, the fact that Hillary was paying her own party at the time, only lent credence to remarks from the likes of Bernie Sanders who stated that a candidate like Hillary was essentially trying to buy an election. But according to party insiders, due to Obama's lack of interest and input, the party needed someone like Hillary to take over.

As the Democratic ship began to sink in wavy political waters, it was Hillary that was able to stay the course. If she bought the election, perhaps she did so more out of necessity than anything else. After Democratic political strategist Donna Brazile took over for Debbie Wasserman Schultz, she too had quite a bit to say about corruption and lack of support in the DNC.

For it was Ms. Brazile's book "Hacks: The Inside Story of the Break-ins and Breakdowns that put Donald Trump in the White House" that served to present a chilling expose on the state of the DNC, from someone who was on the inside.

According to her, since the 2012 election Obama had failed to make any substantial inroads to payoff political debt that had been accrued.

Even worse, rather than own-up to the facts, party officials were either lying or greatly minimizing the problem when asked about the state of party finances.

Things were so bad that the DNC was practically begging for Hillary to take over. And even as more and more DNC operations shifted from Washington and on over to Clinton's New York, hardly anybody batted an eye. It was only when leaked emails between Hillary and former DNC Debbie Wasserman Schultz came out that the rest of the world was filled in.

In Hillary's estimation it was all of these things combined that helped Trump win the presidency. So, taking all of this into consideration, when Trump joked in front of a live audience and pretended to address Russia stating, "Russia if you are listening, see if you could find those missing emails", perhaps he should have said, "Barack Obama if you are listening, thank you for bankrupting the DNC!" Because these many levels of major failures within the DNC could be the real reason Donald Trump was elected in the first place.

CHAPTER 11

Collusion and Delusion

"I have just been informed that the alleged shooter at the Republican baseball practice is someone who apparently volunteered on my presidential campaign. I am sickened by this despicable act. Let me be as clear as I can be. Violence of any kind is unacceptable in our society and I condemn this action in the strongest possible terms. Real change can only come about through nonviolent action, and anything else runs against our most deeply held American values."

–Senator Bernie Sanders

IT WAS ON JANUARY 10th, 2017, just 10 days before President-elect Donald Trump had even been inaugurated into office, that Buzzfeed News published an unverified report known as the Steele dossier.

This report composed by former M16 British intelligence agent, Michael Steele, made allegations that the Trump campaign colluded with Russia. Though the Mueller Report has since established the dossier as meritless, at the time it proved to be an irresistible piece of catnip for the news media.

For a moment, many mainstream news segments including NBC's Nightly News with Lester Holt, were echoing the wild claims in the Steele dossier as if they were completely factual. Though we now know the report was bogus, these same media outlets failed to issue any sort of apology for airing this bit of dirty laundry, they simply just stopped talking about it.

Despite being disproven, the Steele dossier and the idea that Trump colluded with Russia has still managed to linger, at least in the left-wing psyche. This chapter explores the colossal conspiracy theory along with other left-wing delusions that have come to light lately.

There are a few reasons why these thoughts and theories have stuck around for the long haul, but the biggest one by far is simply the continued disbelief in Trump's 2016 win. His victory was so unprecedented, so unpredicted, that for some it wasn't just surprising—it was tremendously traumatizing!

Trump after all, did indeed run a campaign that tended to be viewed as crass and abrasive by some. However, he was an equal opportunity offender in this sense, or as the Republican Governor from Ohio who ran against him plainly put it, "There isn't a person, or group that Donald Trump *hasn't offended.*"

At any rate, when many folks on the Left saw this crude 'vulgarian' seemingly bully and barge his way into the White House, it was apparently hard for them to accept that he had arrived there fairly. So it was that immediately after the ballots were counted, there were many who questioned the validity of the election results and Trump's victory.

With such a perception from the outset, it shouldn't be too surprising that practically every move the Trump administration makes is scrutinized by most mainstream media as well as those who did not vote for him. Though as much as someone might be quick to call conspiracy theory when explaining how an election occurred in a way that was unfavorable to them, we have to warn that when taken too far, these conspiracy theories aren't only potentially dangerous—they can be downright deadly!

It was just a few months after the election, when one particular conspiracy theorist on the left demonstrated just how deadly harboring such twisted beliefs can be. On July 17th, 2017, an unemployed drifter by the name of James T. Hodgkinson armed himself with an assault rifle and made his way into the dugout of a baseball game between politicians.

The game was actually a practice run for an annual fundraising event being held the following day called the Congressional Baseball Game for Charity, which Republican members of the House hold every year. Unfortunately that year, what began as a friendly gathering for a practice session ended in tragedy when Hodgkinson stormed onto the baseball field and started shooting.

In the immediate aftermath 6 people were wounded with 2 of them being critically injured including the assailant and Republican Congressman Steve Scalise. Fortunately, capital police were able to move in and takedown Hodgkinson before he could hurt anyone else.

Hodgkinson would later die of the injuries he sustained that day, leaving only his conspiratorial murmurings on Facebook as testament as to why he did what he did. Since 2011 he was a vocal supporter of the Occupy Wall Street movement and had firmly believed that big corporations had taken over America.

By 2017, these views morphed into his conviction that Trump had somehow hijacked the country. So, soon after the election of Donald Trump, this former Bernie Sanders supporter decided that Trump and anyone associated with him was a dire threat to the nation.

It appears that nobody really took him too seriously, when shortly before he attacked the Republican representatives on that baseball field, he very clearly stated his intent on Facebook. In fact, he posted on his own page, “It’s time to destroy Trump & Co.”

Sadly, due to the venom that is presently poisoning our politics, his post of course received more than a few thumbs up and cheers. Though it’s unlikely that anybody who hit the ‘like’ button ever imagined this disgruntled man literally meant what he said, and that he would take his anger out of the online forums and into real life.

This is the potential danger posed by extreme beliefs and individuals unwilling to compromise any of their own hard-headed viewpoints. Sadly, the sentiment has only increased over the past few years. This was evidenced when Robert Mueller finished up his infamous report on Russian interference in the 2016 election.

The report discovered zero evidence of the Trump campaign conspiring with Russia. After 2 years of extensive investigating they found zip, nada, nothing at all that implicated Donald Trump in colluding with any Russian national whatsoever.

Yet regardless of this vindication (and yes, I would say it qualifies as vindication) those who wanted to believe that Trump had a Russia connection steadfastly refused to believe the hard truth. Some in fact were so confident in the accusations and stuck in their mindset that even to this day, they'll still say he's guilty.

Former Democratic presidential candidate Beto O'Rourke, had painted himself into such a corner. Just a few days before the Mueller Report was to be released, Beto had infamously remarked, "You have a president, who in my opinion, beyond the shadow of a doubt, sought to collude with the Russian government."

There it was, hollered for the whole world to hear, Beto had declared that "in his opinion" Trump/Russia collusion was "beyond the shadow of a doubt" a real thing. Well, his rock-solid *opinion* proved to be entirely wrong. Even so, did you see any apology from Beto or anyone else like him? No, just more conjecture and accusations.

In the immediate aftermath of the findings in the Mueller Report, the Left being unsure of what else to do, grabbed onto the fact that the full report had not been released, and this then became their next rallying call. With Beto himself trying to lead the charge as he shouted from Twitter with all the bravado of a tacky internet meme, "Release the Mueller Report to the American People."

Trump's Attorney General, William Barr, eventually acquiesced to these demands. Yet because certain information had been redacted, primarily out of concerns of endangering ongoing investigations, the Democrats once again cried foul. Now it wasn't good enough to get the full report, they needed a report free of any and all redactions.

Even though not shielding witnesses is technically against the law, the Democrats wanted more. Well, if you have ever heard the story 'If You Give a Mouse a Cookie' , then you know that these democrat rats won't stop until they get a cookie along with a big glass of milk, and more...!

And now here we are with accusations ringing around a phone call that occurred just a couple of months after the requested Mueller Report was released. After being cleared of colluding with Russia, Trump is currently being accused of colluding with Ukraine.

Even though Bob Mueller has all but proven that Trump had nothing to do with Russian meddling in 2016, during the 2019 impeachment trial house democrats openly spoke of Trump colluding with Russia in 2016 and trying to collude with "another foreign power" (Ukraine) in the 2020 elections.

As much as the news media likes to "fact check" Trump and his fellow Republicans, hardly anyone raised an eyebrow at these blatant fabrications. Collusion was all but proven to be a delusion, and yet the lies and accusations against a duly elected president of the United States continue with astonishing abandon.

CHAPTER 12

The Politics of Pivotal Shifts

"The Democrats are the party that says government will make you smarter, taller, richer, and remove the crabgrass on your lawn. The Republicans are the party that says government doesn't work and then they get elected and prove it."
–P.J. O'Rourke

IN THE WORLD OF political science, there is something that analysts refer to as a "pivotal shift." Similar to some rare weather or geological phenomenon; the pivotal shift turns everything on its head, and only occurs about once every generation or so. But what exactly is a pivotal shift in politics?

It's when a political party changes so dramatically that it is no longer recognizable to many of its original constituents. The Democratic Party in particular has gone through a pivotal shift before. All one has to do is consider the fact that the original base of the Democrats were European-American, proslavery southerners known as the Dixiecrats, and their nemesis was an abolitionist Republican named Abraham Lincoln!

By the time of John F. Kennedy in the 1960's however, the ideology of the Democratic Party had shifted quite a bit, and the transformation was complete by the time Kennedy's successor, Lyndon Baines Johnson, took over in the oval office. Then years later in 1992, the Democratic Party began to slightly shift again under the leadership of Bill Clinton.

Bill Clinton ran on jobs and the economy, but the trade deal he championed called "NAFTA" promised to send many of those blue-collar jobs he touted, south of the border to Mexico. The Democratic Party downplayed the concerns over this deal,, suggesting that the future for the American worker was not in jeopardy and would remain strong.

Then Vice President Al Gore even offered a laughable side note, when he suggested that shipping jobs to Mexico would remove the incentive of illegal aliens crossing the border. Yes, he actually stated that the trade deal could "cut down on illegal immigration." Of course, considering the caravans of illegal currently swarming the borders , this proved to be as much of a joke as it sounded at the time.

Nevertheless, Bill Clinton managed to win a 2nd term, but by the time his presidency finally came to a close in the year 2000, many Democrats were maybe just a bit too queasy to stomach supporting his successor, Al Gore. And as close as the election was between Al Gore and George W. Bush, if traditional blue-collar Democrats turned off by the Bill Clinton years had actually shown up at the booths on election day, Gore would have had a decisive win over Bush.

This of course did not happen, and although Gore beat Bush in the popular vote, Bush squeaked out an Electoral College win. Blue Dog Democrats again failed to show up in force for the 2004 elections and Bush won a 2nd term, defeating Senator John Kerry. It wasn't until hope and change arrived with the inspirational and historic candidacy of Barack Obama in the 2008 presidential election that many blue-collar working-class voters were lured back to the Democratic Party.

In 2012 Obama managed to secure a 2nd term for himself, but by the time of the 2016 presidential election, Hillary discovered that she had inherited a sinking ship and many were abandoning it, especially the working class!

Flash forward to 2020 and the Democratic Party seems to be on the verge of another big pivotal shift. Now many more formerly faithful Democratic voters are finding themselves increasingly alienated by platform tenants and seem to view them as too extreme.

This phenomenon has been most visibly demonstrated in recent years with the "Walk Away" movement, which was founded by political activist and former Democrat; Brandon Straka in 2018. Since then, Mr. Straka has been a regular on the talk show circuit, where he is quite vocal about his decision to leave the Democratic Party.

According to Straka, formerly loyal democrats like him are leaving the party in droves because they are sick of what he calls a "toxic and hate filled" environment within the party. They're weary of a group that values "political correctness" more than real solutions.

Are such things a sign that a great exodus of disaffected Democrats is imminent? And if so, after this thinning of the ranks, what will the remnants of the old Democratic Party resemble or become?

Some believe that the prototype of the future Democrats lies with the so-called "Squad." This is a nickname that was given to four newly elected congresswomen who road to office on a wave of progressive fervor during the 2018 midterm elections.

The group has embraced the idea that they represent a younger, more progressive and diverse generation, and have made it part of their mission to actively transform both the platform and the makeup of the traditional Democratic Party.

With the newly elected congresswoman Alexandria Ocasio-Cortez at the helm, the squad has advocated for everything from environmental protection, universal healthcare, and the abolishment of ICE (Immigration and Customs Enforcement), to tuition-free schools and sweeping reform of the criminal justice system.

Whether you agree with them or not, the plans of AOC and the Squad are ambitious to say the least. And helping to keep the wind behind these progressive sails is a little-known political action committee known as the "Justice Democrats." This is a group that was formed by progressives out of the ashes of the 2016 Bernie Sanders campaign.

The stated goal of the Justice Democrats is to "replace every corporate-backed member of Congress" and "rebuild the Democratic Party from scratch" if need be. It's interesting to note that it was out of the spurned and disaffected Bernie Sanders supporters that this progressive new wing of the Democratic Party was born.

It seems that in the wake of Bernie's defeat, his supporters took the phrase, "If you can't beat them, join them" and changed it to, "If you can't beat them, then rebuild it from scratch!" And that is precisely what the Justice Democrats are trying to do, with the progressive clique called the Squad leading the charge,

With a stated goal of disruption like this, veteran Democrats obviously have something to be a bit concerned about. Justice Democrats like AOC are determined to standup to the status quo of their party in order to exact the change they want.

And the Squad has already had several showdowns with their own Democratic leader in the house, Nancy Pelosi. For instance, AOC's proposed resolution called the "Green New Deal" was famously dismissed by Pelosi as "the green dream", maintaining that what AOC and company were asking for was completely preposterous.

Nancy and AOC had another tiff in the summer of 2019 when Cortez and her loyal cohorts voted against a 4.6-billion-dollar border bill that was signed by Donald Trump. This was actually one of the few successful bipartisan pieces of legislation in recent memory, yet the Squad members were the lone holdouts to vote against it.

At the time, Pelosi scoffed at the squad's resistance and ridiculed them, by saying, "All these people have their public whatever and their 'Twitter World.' But they didn't have any following. They're four people and that's how many votes they got."

The bill allocated funds to help treat children and their families who had been detained at the US border. According to other progressives their aim was to provide, necessities such as "food and blankets" while simultaneously putting "guardrails" in place to prevent the president from redirecting funds for border security agencies such as ICE.

But the more radical new progressives didn't want to provide Trump with one penny for border security. The more pragmatic Pelosi realized that she wouldn't be able to get the bill passed, and therefore wouldn't be able to bring that much talked about "food and blankets" to the detained families, unless she was able to get her party to compromise with the president.

However, Alexandria Ocasio-Cortez and company just didn't see it that way. They felt that Nancy was unnecessarily caving in to the pressure, and failing to hold the Trump administration accountable. Others however were quick to point out that the bill gave Democrats most of what they wanted and holding out at this point only served to hurt the detained illegal immigrants who AOC and others claimed they were trying so hard to protect.

At any rate, the bill ultimately passed but the rancor between AOC and Nancy Pelosi did not. Perhaps the biggest fault line of contention between Pelosi and the more vocal factions of the Democratic Party is the 2019 impeachment of President Donald Trump. Nancy Pelosi knowing that impeachment would not be politically expedient and possibly politically damaging during a presidential election year, tried her best to resist the growing calls for impeachment.

At one point she even went on the record to warn fellow Democrats that Donald Trump was practically "goading them" into impeaching him. Nevertheless, the cries for impeachment coming from the Squad and their supporters were so loud and repeating that Nancy Pelosi could no longer resist the request.

And so, on the flimsiest grounds in history, a sitting president was impeached. What can we make of this rather radical new trajectory? Are the Democrats headed directly off a cliff? Or is it just another, long awaited pivotal shift? Only time will tell!

CHAPTER 13

Setting the Political Agenda

"I spend a good portion of my dinner-party conversation defending America because no matter what the political agenda, it's still a fantastic, amazing place."
—Gwyneth Paltrow

A GOOD LAWYER KNOWS that in some sense everything is relative. Not relative in the sense that solid facts and figures can be supplanted with erroneous ones, but relative in how those same said facts are presented and how they are perceived.

We see this kind of shadow play in contemporary politics all the time. A lot of the time when a politician advocates for something, it's not so much that they're trying to present an accurate picture of the facts as it is trying to fit their viewpoint into a narrowly defined narrative.

If something is found not to fit that narrowly defined narrative, it is often either denied or completely omitted. This my friends, is called "setting the agenda." Everyone has an agenda, and career politicians, professional activists, and their supporters in the media have become experts at presenting their one-sided worldviews.

Just take for example the issue of renewable energy. Many environmental groups would want nothing more than to cover all of

North America with giant wind turbines in an effort to produce clean and renewable energy. Electricity from the wind?

Sounds like a great idea, right? The only trouble is—wind turbines are actually pretty bad for the environment. Because while wind turbines are indeed a clean energy source, generating power from a huge set of blades spinning high in the air has the decidedly negative consequence of decimating bird populations.

Unfortunately, flocks of birds fly right into those wind turbines and get chopped to bits. It happens all the time and no one is quite sure how to solve the problem yet. In fact, wind turbines in California currently pose a dire threat to an endangered species.

The California Condor, of which there are now less than a few hundred left in the wild, has also become a victim of the wind turbines spinning blades. So, what did the environmental wing in Washington do in order to address this environmental catastrophe? Did they terminate wind turbine use in California?

Well, since doing that most definitely didn't fit their narrative, they decided to look the other way instead. In 2011, environmentalists lobbied Washington and managed to get the Obama Administration to grant wind farms an exemption when it came to killing the endangered California Condor.

While anyone else who kills a condor, even if by accident, is subject to prosecution, wind turbine farms basically have a license to kill these beautiful endangered birds. The ironic thing is, if it were a polluting smokestack from an industrial factory that was causing birds to drop dead, the environmentalists would be all over it until the place was shutdown

Yet if any aspect of their own prized agenda is responsible for wrongdoing, they rush to cover it up, keep it quiet, and/or solicit government officials to grant them immunity. This is the hypocritical way that many political activists set their agenda.

If it aids their cause, it's a talking point, but if it is negative for the narrative they wish to present, it'll never see the light of day. Political agendas have what political scientists refer to as "priority lists." If any given issue or incident doesn't involve anything on their list of stated agendas, it is disregarded and discarded.

This agenda setting seems to have become much more clear since Donald Trump arrived at the White House. And while Trump himself clearly does set his own political agenda; the lock step agenda of the Left is the most clearly revealed simply in how they respond to this president whom they seem to hold so much animosity for.

A good, though startling example of this is how they respond to Trump's efforts on foreign policy. For instance, consider the potential powder keg of North Korea. When Trump first entered office, he promised to take a strong stance with the North Koreans and was quickly accused of saber rattling.

Never mind the fact that the leader of North Korea, Kim Jong Un, has been rattling his sabre at the United States ever since he took over leadership from his deceased father Kim Jong-il in 2011. Kim has repeatedly threatened the United States with nuclear annihilation and has leveled insults at just about every U.S. official that was ever brought to his attention.

In 2014 he launched an insult at Obama that many deemed to be racially charged when he declared, "Obama always goes reckless in words and deeds like a monkey in a tropical forest." He also apparently had ire for Obama's Secretary of State at the time, John Kerry, whom he said looked like a "wolf with a hideous lantern jaw."

But beyond the absurd insults, Kim Jong Un also commissioned feature length propaganda videos, which seemed to depict North Korean nuclear missiles blowing the White House to smithereens. Kim, the master of misanthropic ceremonies, then openly declared that the nuclear annihilation of the U.S. at the hands of North Korea was imminent.

What did the Obama administration choose to do over this? They exercised restraint, or in sheer layman's terms; *they didn't do anything at all.* Because unlike the aspersions that Kim tried to cast on Obama's character, Obama most certainly wasn't reckless. Whether you agreed with his policy or not, Obama was actually very cautious when it came to the potential use, or even threat of military force.

All one has to do is think back to the Benghazi fiasco in Libya and you can see this hesitation to act played out. Here Obama famously dithered when it came to sending U.S. marines to backup a U.S. embassy threatened by protesters, resulting in the compound being stormed by a mob and Americans including a U.S. ambassador getting killed.

All of this could have been avoided however if Obama would have been assertive enough to order military reinforcements as soon as the incident erupted. Instead, the former law professor cautiously contemplated about the situation, weighed all the options, considered all the factors involved, and perhaps entered into a state of refined reflection.

With all of this fancy philosophical thought going on in Obama's mind, by the time he decided to act, it was too late. So no, Obama is not at all reckless like Kim claimed him to be. If anything, Obama was the opposite of that—he was overly cautious.

And it was precisely this hesitancy to act in the face of Kim Jong Un's provocations that led to such a hamstrung policy when it came to North Korea. Upon Donald Trump's arrival on the scene however, that all changed. And as soon as Kim started acting up under his watch, Trump was quick to attack back and hold him accountable.

He openly warned Kim of what would happen to him if he went too far, suggesting that he and all of North Korea would be wiped out in a conflagration of "fire and fury like the world has never seen." This prompted a response from none other than Trump's former opponent Hillary Clinton who stated that, "cavalier threats to start war on the Korean peninsular are dangerous and short-sighted."

Every other talking head on the liberal Left then quickly followed suite, outraged that Trump would breakaway from their agenda of ignoring the dictator and dare to call Kim's blustering bluff. Clinton also weighed in on a series of taunts between the two men, in which Kim called Trump an "Old Dotard" (whatever that means?) and Trump ridiculed Kim (the guy obsessed with rocket tests) by calling him "Little Rocket Man."

Hillary claimed that "the insults on Twitter" were only going to make "future negotiations with North Korea difficult." In other words, Trump needed to just shut-up, ignore Kim's insults, and hope and pray the North Koreans would suddenly come to the table in peace.

Though this strategy has never really worked in the past, Hillary thought it would somehow work in the future. They say that insanity is doing the same thing over and over while expecting a different result, yet this is what Hillary's recommendations for Donald Trump were regarding the situation.

Furthermore, she believed that Trump standing up for himself would put any future talks in jeopardy. Really? It makes one wonder what Clinton thought when Trump successfully brought Kim to the negotiation table for a historic meeting in 2018.

Trump seemed to do the impossible, when no other U.S. president was able to gain access to the isolated North Korean leader, Trump sat him down and had a frank discussion face to face. That was about one year after Hillary and her associates claimed that Trump's antics were going to jeopardize "future negotiations" with North Korea.

And now that Trump was speaking directly, in person with the infamous dictator, instead of hailing it as a breakthrough moment, the Liberal talking heads and their friends in the media suddenly changed course and spoke as if it were all a bad thing.

Instead of being worried that Trump might "offend" the despot and mess up any chances of future negotiations, they now insisted that it was highly inappropriate to see Trump "cozying up to a dictator."

In reality, it simply doesn't fit the Left's agenda if Trump is successful in any foreign policy. So, when actual good comes from his efforts, they are almost always going to somehow turn a positive into a negative. One day they could be lambasting him for being too aggressive with Kim Jong Un, and then the very next day they're criticizing him for being too nice.

Trump seems to shine a light on the underhanded tactics of the Democratic Party in ways that few others ever have or could. Political parties do indeed have an agenda; it's just never been so blatantly obvious as it is today. The only way the American people can reverse the trends of agendas set by politicians is to reverse our support at the ballot box. Because in the end, it is the American people who will ultimately set the political agenda with their votes.

CHAPTER 14

Thinking Outside the Washington Box

"It isn't enough to think outside the box. Thinking is passive. Get used to acting outside the box."
–TIMOTHY FERRISS

DONALD TRUMP, ANDREW YANG, and Kanye West—what do all three of these people have in common? Well, one is a duly elected president, another is currently running for president, and the third has announced plans to run in 2024. Plus, they all came onto the political scene as Washington outsiders!

Some may find it amusing to even mention the outspoken rapper Kanye West in this grouping, but the idea of someone like West pursuing the presidency isn't as preposterous as it seemed just a few years ago. And seemingly inspired by Trump's success, the hip-hop mastermind truly believes that he too can successfully run and become elected to the highest office in the land. And quite honestly—anything is possible at this point!

Because whether you like or dislike President Trump, his electoral success shattered one of the greatest barriers in society. I'm not talking about the glass ceiling; I'm talking about the barrier of prior political experience. Although it's not likened in these terms very often, the presidency of Donald Trump is indeed historic.

Trump after all is the very first person to be elected president with no prior political or even military experience. All previous presidents have either been former vice presidents, governors, senators, or four-star generals. Trump was a wealthy real estate developer from New York and now he's president of the United States, which has never happened before. Most of the time having accumulated vast experience in a certain field is considered a positive thing, and this is the way that American politics was handled for many years.

But in more recent times, Americans have grown weary of career politicians who impose their 'Washington Values' on the rest of the nation. It is the fatigue felt by our weary electorate over these more established political figures that has led Americans to yearn for those who might think a bit outside of the Washington Box.

It is in this sort of climate, that someone who claims to be a Washington outsider with little to no experience can actually have an edge over more experienced political candidates. This is precisely what happened for Donald Trump in the 2016 election, in which he defeated GOP standard bearers such as Jeb Bush and John Kasich with ease.

He did so not by touting any previous legislative experience, but by touting his business acumen and continually insisting that he had more common sense than the current crop of political aspirants that he shared the debate stage with. And Trump had done his homework; he knew the issues in many cases better than the veterans and therefore was able to present a cohesive set of speaking points that connected with the average voter.

Even if they don't agree with his policies, many other successful businessmen, CEO's, celebrities, and moguls have been inspired by Trump's efforts to enter into the political arena. Yang has even actively campaigned to take Trump's core voters that Hillary Clinton christened as Trump's "basketful of deplorables", as his own.

For those such as Hillary, who theorized that Trump's support base was comprised mostly of deplorable racists and sexists, some such as Andrew Yang see things differently. Yang believes the real reason Trump gained the support of so many people was because a desperate working-class electorate were tired of losing jobs due to the actions and incompetence of the Washington establishment.

He believes that they placed their bets on Trump (a decided outsider) to work as a wrecking ball against the political elites that they felt had led them into such dire straits. Yang however, believes Trump in the end isn't the answer, and he is calling on this key group of Trump voters to support him instead.

He reminds them that he too is an outsider as a tech executive in Silicon Valley, but he knows better than almost anyone how jobs are being lost on a daily basis. However, he doesn't blame illegal immigration or the fact that some of the manufacturing jobs have gone oversees.

Because as Yang sees it, the biggest threat to factory jobs isn't that they are being outsourced to other countries, it's that they are being completely displaced by new developments in robotics and AI. As Yang points out, we already see retail jobs such as that of being a cashier soon becoming obsolete due to self-checkout lanes.

Call centers are equally being bled of workers in light of Artificially Intelligent customer service. Yang has been acutely aware of the displacement that new technology poses for the American worker, and warns that the next major shift will be when self-driving cars and trucks cause the loss of gainful employment for millions of taxi, delivery, and truck drivers.

Yang has gone on the record to state that Trump has correctly identified many of the problems in society such as the loss of jobs for the working class—he just isn't finding the right solutions. But apparently even pointing out that Trump "got the problems right" is a cardinal sin for hard-line democrats who gasp at any suggestion of Trump getting anything right.

Democrats are also upset that Yang has appeared as a guest on conservative programming, like when he did an interview with Tucker

Carlson. By and large the Democratic establishment has not been friendly to the candidacy of Andrew Yang, and this rancour has only increased as he continues to maintain his public support.

Is the democratic establishment afraid that they have another disrupter like Donald Trump on their hands? (Except this time coming out of the Left) It would seem so. Yang has indeed been likened as a "dangerous outsider" and much of the mainstream media coverage of him has not been all too favorable.

When a recent poll revealed that 10% or more of current Donald Trump voters would vote for Andrew Yang, you would think Democrats would view this as a good thing. Usually parties are thrilled to know that they have candidates that could steal votes from their constituents. But rather than this being a badge of honour, they placed these findings on Yang's back as if it were a pollster placard of shame.

The current incarnation of Democrats is still so stringently against all things Trump and his status as a Washington outsider, (and even the voters that put him into office) that they can't even stand the idea of one of their own candidates gleaning some of this wellspring of support.

Yang has since spoken of this cold shoulder he believes he's getting. As recently as December of 2019, he complained that the DNC was not conducting adequate polling in order to ensure all the candidates received a fair shake. He requested additional polling ahead of the primaries but was roundly rejected.

Nevertheless, Yang continues to ride on a wave of popular support that seems to transcend partisan boundaries. Despite the speed bumps that the media and members of his own chosen political party have put in place, this Washington outsider is garnering a lot of interest for his straight talk and pledges to reach across the aisle.

Many voters certainly do admire candidates like Andrew Yang who are willing to think outside of the Washington box. With the election of Donald Trump, voters have made it very clear that they are tired of the same old crop of candidates that the political machine yields. They desire someone that goes beyond the dirty game of identity politics that has been used to so bitterly divide the electorate as well as the general public.

They want someone who is willing to step away from the old political talking points of the party platform in order to offer real solutions to real problems. Yes, many voters today certainly do admire and desire a candidate like Andrew Yang, who is ready and willing to think outside of the Washington box!

CONCLUSION

Where Do We Go from Here?

THE CHAPTERS OF THIS book have navigated through some of the murkier waters in America's political environment. But we're going to end it on a bright note and despite all the doom and gloom focus on some of the positives that can be found. Is there light at the end of the political spectrum here in the United States?

Yes, there surely is! For one thing, the American electorate is going through changes and a new generation is now rising up and learning how to make use of tools that previous generations could only have dreamed of. Millennials and others are using social media like never before in order to get their point across, and they have become quite savvy at doing so!

The younger generations have developed the mind of a critical thinker as a default. Rather than depending on everything the New York Times tells them, they conduct online searches, and do their own fact checking to discover the truth for themselves.

The days of depending on the 6 o'clock news to give it to you straight are unfortunately over, and have been for some time. The electorate of the future is not only highly informed, but they are experts at disseminating that information in such a way that they can make their own logical conclusions.

Dishonest politicians, media, and faulty narratives have dug a deep political hole for our country in recent years, but the current crop of Americans is more than capable of digging us out.

The older generations often look down on the younger as not living up to the standards that have been set before them. The "Greatest Generation" of the World War II era, regularly looked down on their baby boomer children as selfish, ungrateful troublemakers.

Generation Xer's were in turn perceived as lazy, apathetic slackers with no direction in life. And now that the millennials have come to the fore, they are routinely lambasted as weak crybabies or 'snowflakes'—the recipients of many "participation awards" who have been helicopter parented so badly that they can't do anything for themselves.

But this actually couldn't be further from the truth. Beyond the negative generational stereotypes, many among the younger generations have been found to be highly intelligent, caring, and thoughtful individuals who are willing to breakup the status quo in order to bring about real and meaningful change.

In concluding this book, I would have to say that despite all of the doom and gloom we hear day in and day out about the political situation in America, there is indeed light at the end of the political spectrum. Because unlike the division seen between Baby Boomers and Generation X, millennials stand fairly united on a wide range of issues.

Whether it's over the environment, immigration, the economy, or social issues, millennials from all walks of life are forming an impressive coalition consisting of Americans from every background, gender, age, race, and occupation.

This gives me some hope that we can indeed discover a way out of the contentious political pit we're presently in. So, where do we go from here or even begin? As glib as it may sound—we must simply keep moving forward! Because as dire as things may seem right now, in reality they are more than likely just the growing pains of our great nation.

Though we've hit a bit of a rough patch, the good news is that it can only get smoother from here! And as bad as the 2010's may have been, in some ways, the 2020's do promise to be much better in many ways. Thanks to the increased interest and awareness of the American electorate, I truly believe that we can all look forward to a brighter and better-informed future, at least when it comes to politics and media in society.

Reference & Further Reading

AS WE BRING THIS book to a close, I would like to share with you some of the reading and reference materials that helped to make this manuscript possible. Here you will find a wide variety of sources that have covered the full spectrum of the issues presented in these pages. Feel free to check them out for yourself.

Attkisson, S. (2017). The Smear: *How Shady Political Operatives and Fake News Control What You See, What You Think, and How You Vote*: HarperCollins Publishers Inc.

Bailyn, B. (1992). *The Ideological Origins of the American Revolution*, Cambridge, MA: Harvard University Press.

Brazile, D. (2017). Hacks: *The Inside Story of the Break-Ins and Breakdowns That Put Donald Trump in the White House,* New York, NY: Hachette Books.

Carlson, T. (2019). Ship of Fools: *How a selfish ruling class is bringing American to the brink of revolution*. New York, NY: Free Press and Imprint of Simon & Schuster, Inc.

Chaffetz, J. (2018). *The Deep State: How an army of bureaucrats protected Barack Obama and is working to destroy Donald Trump*. New York, NY: Broadside Books.

Chozick, A (March 25, 2019). *After Mueller Report, News Media Leaders Defend Their Work. http://www.nytimes.com*

Coulter, A.H. (2012). Demonic: *How the Liberal Mob is Endangering America.* New York, NY: Crown Forum.

Dengor, P. (2006). *The Crusader: Ronald Reagan and the Fall of Communism.* New York, NY: Harper Perennial.

Dewey, J. (1927). *The Public and Its Problems.* Athens, Ohio: University Press.

Edwards, L. (2018). *The FBI Spied for LBJ's Campaign.* www.heritage.org

Folson, W.F. Jr. (2006). *FDR and the IRS.* www.hillsdale.edu

Gingrich, N. (2018). *Understanding Trump.* New York, NY: Center Street.

Holzer, H. (2014). *Lincoln and the Power of the Press.*

New York: Simon & Schuster.

House Judiciary Committee (1974). *Articles of Impeachment.* http://watergate.info/impeachment/articles-of-impeachment

House Judicial Committee (2019). *Articles of Impeachment.* https://assets.documentcloud.org/documents/6572310/Text-Articles-of-Impeachment-Against-President.pdf

Humphrey, C.S. (2013). *The American Revolution and the Press.* Evanston, IL: Northwestern University Press.

Hutchins Commission (1947). *A Free and Responsible Press, A General Report on Mass Communication: News, Radio, Motion Pictures, Magazines and Books, Commission on Freedom of the Press.* University of Chicago Press.

Knight Foundation (September 2018). *Indicators of News Media Trust,* A Gallup/Knight Foundation Survey

https://kfsiteproduction.s3.amazonaws.com/media_elements/files/000/000/216/original/KnightFoundation_Panel4_Trust_Indicators_FINAL.pdf

Kuypers, J.A. (2014). *Partisan Journalism,* Lanham, MD: Rowman & Littlefield.

Levin, M.R. (2019). *Unfreedom of the Press,* New York, NY: Threshold Editions / A threshold of Simon & Schuster, Inc.

Lofgren, M. (2016). The Deep State: *The fall of the Constitution and the rise of a shadow government.*

Penguin Group USA.

Onuf, P., *Thomas Jefferson: Campaigns and Elections*

https://millercenter.org/president/jefferson/campaigns-and-elections

Paine, T. (February 1776). *Common Sense.*

http://www.ushistory.org/paine/commonsense/

Parnes, J. & Allen, A. (2015). HRC: *State Secrets and the Rebirth of Hillary Clinton.* Random House UK.

Patterson, T.E. (May 18, 2017). *News coverage of Donald Trump's First 100 Days,* Harvard Kennedy School, Shorenstein Center on Media, Politics, and Public Policy. https://shorensteincenter.org/news-coverage-donald-trump-first-100-days

Payne, D. (2017). 16 Fake News Stories Reporters Have Run Since Trump Won. https://thefederalist.com

Shafer, J. & Doherty,T. (May/June 2017).

The Media Bubble Is Worse than You Think

www.politico.com/magazine/story/2017/04/25/media_bubble-real-journalism-jobs-eash-coast-215048

Wilson, Woodrow (2008). *Fourth of July Address on the Declaration of Independence*, appearing in Classics of American Political & Constitutional Thought, vol.2, Cambridge, MA: Hackett

U.S. Constitution, (1965). The *Twenty-fifth Amendment*

About the Author

WILLIAM M. FRASER

WILLIAM M. FRASER, passionate outdoorsman who enjoys travelling and spending time with friends, family and their pet dogs when not focusing on his research in the public policy arena

STAY CONNECTED

Like my Facebook page to get updates, fun, and prizes!

Purchase this book:
https://buy.bookfunnel.com/qq2v3jvex5

Made in the USA
Monee, IL
08 November 2026

67994726R00080